GREAT AMERICAN

FOR
JAMES BEARD
AND JULIA CHILD,
WHO LIT THE LAMP
AND SHOWED US
THE WAY

COOKING SCHOOLS

GREAT AMERICAN COOKING SCHOOLS

Fair Game
A HUNTER'S COOKBOOK

JANE HIBLER

ILLUSTRATED BY SANDRA CIARROCHI

IRENA CHALMERS COOKBOOKS, INC. • **NEW YORK**

IRENA CHALMERS COOKBOOKS, INC.

PUBLISHER
Irena Chalmers

Managing Editor
Jean Atcheson

Sales and Marketing Director
Diane J. Robbins

Series Design
Helene Berinsky

Cover Design
Milton Glaser
Karen Skelton, *Associate Designer*

Cover Photography
Matthew Klein

Editor for this book
Betsy Lawrence

Typesetting
Acu-Type Services, Clinton, CT

Printing
John D. Lucas Printing Co., Baltimore, MD

Editorial Offices
23 East 92nd Street
New York, NY 10128
(212) 289-3105

Sales Offices
P.O. Box 988
Denton, NC 27239
(800) 334-8128 or
(704) 869-4518 (NC)

ISBN #0-94-1034-15-1

Printed and published in the United States of America
by Irena Chalmers Cookbooks, Inc.

LIBRARY OF CONGRESS
CATALOG CARD NO.: 83-071039
    Hibler, Jane.
       Fair game: a hunter's cookbook
    New York, NY: Chalmers, Irena Cookbooks, Inc.
84 p.

F G H I J   8 7 6 5 4   595/10

Contents

Acknowledgments

I would like to express special thanks to Irena Chalmers for giving me the opportunity to publish this book; to my husband for his endless supply of wild game and, more importantly, for his constant encouragement; to my parents, Jim and Kassie Franke, for educating my palate; to my son Kelly, whose first buck provided much of the venison that I tested recipes on; to my daughter Kristin, who patiently ate game, night after night, and who now requests that I write a book on desserts; to Jim Sehon, Jim and Kim Maybry, Annette and David Butler and Lee Hibler for their contributions of wild game for recipe testing; to Ken Durbin of the Oregon Department of Fish and Wildlife for his helpful information; to Renée Glasgow for her editing assistance; to Pamela Dunn and Sue Ferris for their editing and typing; and lastly, to the Boucock family for their friendship and many memorable hunting seasons on their ranch.

The patron saint of all hunters is St. Hubert, an 8th-century French bishop. The story goes that, while hunting in the forest on Good Friday, he came across a stag bearing between its antlers a cross surrounded by rays of light, and at once fell on his knees in pious adoration. The legend inspired many medieval artists and sculptors, among them the architect of St. Hubert's Chapel in the Chateau d'Amboise in the Loire region of France, where the saint's miraculous encounter with the stag is shown above the entrance and the chapel steeple rises from a thicket of stone antlers.

Introduction

From the beginning of man's life on earth, hunting has been one of the most important factors in our survival. It has provided us with game to feed our families, hides for shelters and clothing, bones and antlers for tools and dishes, sinew for hunting weapons, thread for sewing and fat for cooking. Over thousands of years, our hunting skills and tools became more sophisticated as our intelligence developed. This increase in capabilities allowed us to become more selective in our choice of game to hunt as our chances of survival increased.

As recently as the end of the 19th century, our North American forebears survived by living off the land. "A man really didn't need much money then, if he lived in the back country," recalled a writer in the *Oregon Journal* in 1927. "Unlike the city dweller, we had no bills to pay for wood, water, light, rent, meat, fish, berries or vegetables. The streams were full of trout. Deer, bear and grouse were plentiful. We raised all the potatoes and other vegetables we needed, as well as chickens, eggs and honey. Our cows furnished us veal, milk and butter. We lived the simple life." Only within the last hundred years in this country has hunting ceased to be a necessity for survival and become a sport.

Coincidentally, it was just a little over one hundred years ago that the first legislation was passed to set aside land for preservation. Yellowstone National Park was made America's first National Park in 1872. It was, in fact, created mainly to protect the geysers and hot springs, and it was not until 1894 that Congress passed a game protection law to fine game poachers.

Theodore Roosevelt was the first president of the United States to set aside national lands for game refuges. In 1904 he created 51 of these, and in 1905 he established the U.S. Forest Service, which in turn set aside large parcels of forest land to help preserve our forests and herds of large game animals.

In three decades, a critical problem emerged. The herds and flocks of animals multiplied at such a fast rate that they overpopulated the land reserves, and the animals began to starve. In the 1930s the American naturalist Aldo Leopold pioneered the concept of ecology, the interrelation of organisms and their environment. Leopold realized that while wolves and other predators benefited the large game herds by culling out the weak and disabled, there were still more animals than food available. His ideas helped generate the management organizations that safeguard the delicate balance in the survival of our wildlife today.

The 1930s also saw legislation that benefited migratory birds. Two federal laws were passed which placed a tax on hunting licenses and ammunition, and the Duck Stamp Law was enacted, requiring all duck hunters over the age of 16 to purchase a duck stamp every year. Revenue generated from these taxes has gone toward the purchasing, maintenance and improvement of wildlife refuge areas. In fact, one good way for non-hunters to contribute to wildlife refuges is to buy a yearly duck stamp.

Today, thanks to the foresight of previous generations, game regions in this country are widespread. Over one-third of the land in the United States, approximately 755 million acres, is publicly owned, and supervised, by federal agencies. Another 75 million acres are owned and maintained by state conservation agencies. Elk, a species on the way to extinction by the turn of the century, now roam the forest areas in parts of Oregon, Northern California, Wyoming, Montana, Idaho, Minnesota, Maine and near the Great Lakes.

A wealth of migratory birds can be found along the Atlantic, Mississippi, Central and Pacific flyways, the established flying routes of migratory birds. The U.S. Fish and Wildlife Service estimates that more than 100 million ducks, geese and swans use these flyways each fall, migrating to warmer southern climates. Upland game as well as small game abound in grain fields all over the continent, having adjusted well to the encroachments of mankind.

The best source of hunting information in your area is your State Department of Fish and Wildlife. Several times a year these agencies publish listings of the state game regulations along with the dates and locations of the various hunting seasons. These brochures are free and can usually be found at stores that sell hunting equipment.

Hunting permits can also be purchased at sporting goods stores, as can any special clothing you might need for your hunting expeditions. For large game hunting, your clothing should be brightly colored to distinguish the hunter from the hunted. For bird hunting, just the opposite, for the hunter wants to be as inconspicuous as possible. My husband likes to tell the story of two would-be duck hunters he and his hunting partner saw one day on a lake west of Eugene, Oregon. The two men were duck hunting out of a bright red canoe and, to make matters worse, they had tied their decoys to the back of the boat and were pulling them along behind.

Whatever species of game lures you to the great outdoors, always practice "hunter's safety" and obey all hunting regulations. These rules guard against the extinction of our prized wildlife and without them, our grandchildren and great-grandchildren might never know the memorable taste of a plump roasted mallard or of a juicy pan-fried elk steak. The survival of hunting as a sport depends on you.

I hope that the recipes in this book will provide you with many hours of enjoyment around your dining table, eating food from America's magnificent bounty of game.

Food For Thought

The *elk* is also called *wapiti,* which is a Shawnee Indian name meaning "white rump." The bull elk is the most polygamous deer in America, and has harems of up to 60 cows.

The *bull moose* is the largest game animal in North America. Moose is an Algonquin Indian word meaning "twig eater."

Caribou is a Micmac Indian word meaning "shoveler." The caribou has the habit of pawing through deep snow to reach its food.

The *jackrabbit* is named after the donkey because of its long ears. It is actually a hare and not a rabbit, because its young are born fully furred with their eyes open.

The *sage grouse* is physically the largest member of the grouse family found in North America.

The *chukar partridge* was originally brought to the United States from Nepal. It is the bird most commonly used in cock fights.

The *gray partridge* or European partridge is also called the Hungarian partridge because it was first imported to America from Hungary.

The *wood duck's* official name is *Aix sponsa. Sponsa* means "betrothed" in Latin, as if this beautifully plumed bird were dressed for its wedding.

The *canvas-back duck* was named after the fine gray and white vermiculations on its back, which resemble the weave in a piece of canvas.

The *green-winged teal* is the smallest American duck.

The *Canada Goose (Branta canadensis)* has four subspecies: Western Canada Goose, Lesser Canada Goose, Crackling Goose and Richardson's Goose.

The *mallard* is the common ancestor of all the domestic ducks in the Northern Hemisphere.

The *pintail duck,* named after its long central tail feathers, and also called a sprig, is the most widely distributed duck in North America.

The *American widgeon* is also called a baldpate and poacher. Not liking to dive, it steals or poaches the roots of wild celery from other diving ducks.

The *bobwhite quail,* widely distributed in the East, is named for its distinctive "bob-bob-white" call.

The smallest upland game bird is the *mourn-*

ing dove, so named for its plaintive call. The birds are also known as turtle doves.

The *wild turkey* is a descendant of the Mexican wild turkey, which the Spanish conquistadors found being raised by the Aztecs.

The *woodcock,* a lesser snipe, is also called a timberdoodle, night partridge, Labrador twister, big-eye, mud snipe and bog sucker.

The only state without a *game refuge* is West Virginia, known for its beautiful wild terrain and somewhat sparse population.

The *Migratory Bird Treaty of October 1918* limits the length of the hunting seasons and the numbers of birds that can be bagged. It was signed by both Great Britain and the United States.

The *Boone and Crockett Club* was formed in 1888. It was founded by Theodore Roosevelt to fight for military protection of the public forests, and named after two of his heroes, Daniel Boone and Davy Crockett. It consisted of 100 scientists, politicians and military men who were all hunters themselves.

Handling Game

One of the key elements in successful game cookery is proper handling from the field to the freezer or frying pan. Certain basic rules apply for all kinds of game, from elk to partridge, while each type of game also requires the use of specific techniques. All game needs to be cooled down as soon as possible to prevent spoiling, and many benefit from immediate dressing. Methods for dressing, cooling and storing vary, however. The following are suggested methods of handling the various kinds of game.

Large Game

Hunters do best to kill large game animals with an accurate shot through the neck. This accomplishes an immediate kill with very little waste of edible meat. After the kill, proper handling of the meat is essential to preserve its finest qualities.

If the animal is field-dressed immediately (the liver, lungs and heart removed), bleeding is not necessary, although it is still advisable. Gutting and skinning the animal as soon as possible after the kill allows the inside of the animal to cool, decreasing the chance of spoilage.

Many hunters prefer to gut the animal immediately but to leave the skin on to protect the carcass until they get home. Once the animal is dressed, skinned and placed in a deer bag, it is critical to keep it chilled by hanging it in a cool room at about 40 degrees Fahrenheit. Hanging the game diminishes the chance of spoilage and allows enzymes to soften and tenderize the meat. In this process, juices are released, altering both the texture and flavor of the venison. The length of time an animal should be hung is a controversial issue among hunters; it varies from two days to two weeks, depending on the animal's size and age and the temperature of the room in which it is hung. We hang our venison an average of five days. With experience, you will be able to judge when your deer has aged to your satisfaction.

If you butcher the deer at home, bone the venison and remove all the fat, as it has a strong, gamey taste. Save the scraps of meat that are too small for stew. They can be used at a later date for hamburger, sausage, jerky or mincemeat. If you wish to make your own venison hamburger, use a ratio of 20 percent pork fat to 80 percent meat; for sausage, use a ratio of 33 percent venison, 33 percent pork and 33 percent pork fat.

Venison steaks can be cut 1/4 inch to 3/4 inch thick, depending upon your own preference. For a family of four, I wrap the steaks in 1½-pound packages. Roasts should weigh from 4 to 6 pounds. I prefer steaks to roasts, so all of our roasts are cut into steaks. Stew meat should be cut into 1-inch or 1½-inch cubes. I put 2 pounds of stew meat in a package, which easily makes enough stew for four to six people.

Once cut, the meat should be double-wrapped in freezer paper and labeled with the date and cut of meat. If it is frozen and maintained at 15 degrees Fahrenheit, or lower, it will keep up to one year without losing any of its fine flavor. Venison hamburger and sausage should be eaten within three to four months because the quality of the fat begins to deteriorate.

For more detailed information on cutting up your animal, write to your state game department or your state university agricultural extension service. Their listings can be found in your telephone directory.

I find it helpful to know something about the physiology of meat before cooking it. Basically, all meat is composed of lean muscle, fatty tissue and connective tissue. The muscles consist of small bundles of muscle cells held together by connective tissue which also contains fat. The muscle itself is more tender than the connective tissue. As an animal grows older it develops more connective tissue, making it tougher than a younger animal. There is also a large amount of connective tissue near the end of a muscle to form the tendon that attaches the muscle to the bone. To understand this easily, examine a shank. The center of the muscle is tender, while the ends of the cut, where there is a large amount of connective tissue, are tough. The size of the muscle and the amount of connective and fatty tissue vary, even within species, with age, sex and nutrition.

Small Game Animals

Small game hunting requires just as much accuracy and skill from the hunter as does large game hunting. Rabbits and hares that dart and dive in the underbrush are tricky targets. Once shot, however, small game are much less cumbersome to handle than larger animals. Packing out a three-pound rabbit is a small task compared to disposing of a 500-pound elk.

Small game animals should be drawn and allowed to cool as soon as possible after having been shot. Once you have arrived home, small game can be skinned. Leaving the fur on the animal during traveling protects the carcass from dirt and insects.

Once the animal has been drawn and skinned, it is ready for the freezer. It should be double-wrapped airtight in freezer paper and frozen immediately. Small game can be kept for up to a year frozen at 15 degrees Fahrenheit.

Birds

For practical purposes birds are divided into three main classifications: upland game birds, migratory birds and shore birds. Hunters should follow a few basic rules for all birds. Once they have been shot, keep them as cool as possible and eviscerate as soon as possible to decrease the chance of spoilage. Any puncturing of the digestive tract by BBs releases the bacteria normally found in the intestine. These bacteria multiply rapidly at warm temperatures and spoil the meat.

There are several different methods for removing the feathers. You can pluck birds either dry or moist. Dry plucking is the easiest, but certain fowl with delicate flesh, such as geese, require plucking after the birds have been dipped in warm sudsy water. If you

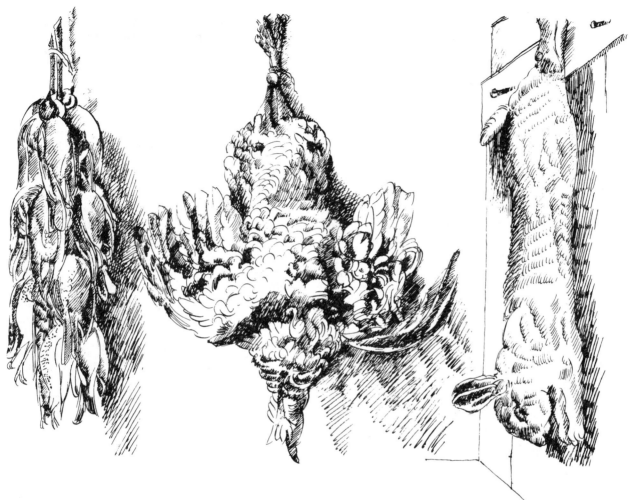

pluck the feathers, pull the feathers in the direction they grow to avoid tearing the skin. Skinning is the preferred method for some birds, such as pheasant, which have such delicate skin that they are almost impossible to pluck. Invariably, skinned birds need to be cooked in a sauce or with butter, oil, or bacon fat to keep them moist.

If you plan on hanging your birds, do it before plucking or skinning. Hanging serves two purposes: to develop the flavor of the bird and to tenderize the meat. Enzymes are released when animals are hung or aged, which break down the tissue and release juices.

After the birds have been drawn, hung and skinned or plucked, they are ready to be cooked or frozen. Skinned birds should be thoroughly wrapped airtight in plastic wrap, then double-wrapped in freezer paper and frozen at 15 degrees Fahrenheit, or lower. They will keep at this temperature for up to a year before they begin to lose their flavor.

Upland Game

Upland game birds should be cooled in a single layer. Once the birds are drawn and cooled, they can be placed in plastic bags and quickly frozen. Many hunters who hunt out of town rent a small freezer locker nearby to store their game.

The older the game bird or any animal, the more connective tissue it will have and consequently the tougher it will be when cooked. Try to determine the age of a bird before it is plucked or skinned. It can then be properly labeled when you are readying it for the freezer, and the older birds can be either braised or stewed.

A quick examination of these colorful birds will reveal clues to their age. The young cocks or male pheasants have a spur on the back of their legs that is pliable and blunt at the end. Adult cocks have spurs that are firm and pointed at the ends. Both young pheasant and grouse have more pliable bills than older birds. If you pick the bird up by its lower jaw and it breaks, you will know that the bird is young. Young partridges have a breastbone that breaks easily and for a time have yellow rather than blue-gray feet.

Many hunters like to age their upland game birds. If you choose to do this, hang the birds unplucked, by the neck, in a cool place—and be sure they are out of reach of a hungry dog, cat or raccoon. I know of one raccoon who rightly hid behind his mask after greedily devouring two of our plump ring-necked pheasants!

In cold weather, game birds can hang up to 10 days; in damp and warm weather, only 3 or 4 days. The aging process is not a rigid procedure and is really a matter of individual taste, which can only be developed by you.

Upland game birds can be either skinned or plucked. If you pluck them, be sure to pull the feathers out in the direction that they grow. If you pull them in the opposite direction, you may tear the skin.

Waterfowl

The flavor of wild birds is solely dependent upon their diet. Because a duck stores its food in its esophagus, the flavor of the food is absorbed into the bloodstream. Not all waterfowl is fishy-tasting, however. The flavor of wild duck will vary, depending upon whether its diet consists of marine life (clams, fish, snails) or vegetation (seeds, sprouts, corn), or a combination of both. The birds with the finest flavor, such as mallard, usually have a diet composed of about 90 percent vegetation. Some ducks, such as widgeon or canvasback, will eat marine life or vegetation, depending on where they find themselves. If you shoot a widgeon at the coast, it will probably taste fishy, but if you shoot it inland, it will be delicious.

To avoid an unpleasant mistake, identify the species and its probable diet before you start plucking. If it is a fish-eating bird, it can be wrapped and labeled as such before freezing. Many cookbooks suggest soaking a "fishy" bird in an acidic solution such as wine or water mixed with lemon juice or vinegar. Although this may help to mask the fishy flavor, nothing will completely eradicate this characteristic taste.

Most of the hunters I know do not hang their waterfowl, but if you choose to, they can be aged for as brief a time as 24 hours, for a young bird, up to more than a week, if the weather is cool. Europeans generally age their birds longer than Americans and Canadians, which produces a much more intense, "high" flavor.

A Word of Advice to Non-Hunters

If there is one thing that all hunters have in common apart from hunting stories, it is the feeling of excitement in the anticipation of the opening of hunting season. If you are not a hunter, don't be confused when hunters talk about opening weekend.

Opening weekend to the hunter is like the weekend after Thanksgiving to the retailer. It is what everyone waits for all year long. Wives who for the past year have fruitlessly begged their husbands to take time to shop for new clothes are astonished to discover, the day before hunting season opens, that not only have the said husbands bought the required hunting license, but they have also shopped for a new deer bag, rifle shells, long underwear, plastic tarps and new scope covers, have filled the propane tank for the camp stove, and have arranged for the necessary days off from work. And have you ever known a hunter to oversleep on opening weekend?

Several years ago I had the opportunity to experience first-hand the opening of deer season with our family of four and another couple. Before we left, it sounded so poetic: two nights in our friend's homestead cabin in the middle of virgin fir country in western Oregon, food cooked on an old wood stove and the crisp autumn air to greet us on our walks in the woods.

On returning home, exhausted, after the big weekend, I looked back over the three days of torrential downpour, and thought of the child who had fallen out of the bunk bed onto his head at 2 A.M., the other child who had walked into a wasps' nest, and the mice that had spent the dark hours of each night scurrying from one end of the cabin to the other. From now on, I concluded, opening weekend for me would be spent in front of my own fireplace in a comfortable chair, reading a good book. You may perhaps want to follow my example.

Several years ago, on the last day of a deer season when hardly an animal had been seen, let alone shot, my husband finally shot a very small forked horn just before sunset. Frustrated and worn out from trudging through the brush, he arrived home and hung the tiny deer in its game bag in the cool shop. Our five-year-old neighbor stole in to marvel and came out with the comment: "Gee, Mr. Hibler, I didn't know deer have wishbones on their heads!"

Helpful Hints

● Before serving game birds to your guests, warn them to beware of an occasional shot that may be lurking in the flesh. Sometimes, if the shots are close to the surface, they can be removed with tweezers before cooking.

● Always wait to stuff game birds until just before they are going to be cooked. Birds filled with a warm stuffing and left to sit for several hours provide perfect conditions for the growth of harmful bacteria.

● Tart fruit and dark game meat go well together. Light game meat, such as pheasant or rabbit, can be accompanied by fruit with a higher sugar content, such as grapes or prunes. Never serve game with overly sweet sauces.

● The fine flavor of game is special and unique. Never cook it with overpowering wines and liquors.

● Because fresh herbs are often difficult to find, all the recipes in this book call for dried herbs. If you do have fresh herbs, by all means use them, adding three times as much of the fresh herb as you would of the dried.

● Dried herbs should always be purchased whole, if possible, because they retain their flavor longer. Crush the herbs in the palm of your hand before adding them to the dish.

● I cook game in heavy cast-iron cookware, either enameled or the plain old-fashioned variety. Almost any cookware will work, but the heavier the pan, the less likely it is that the game will burn.

● The clay pot is a wonderful asset in the kitchen of a game cook. The steam given off during cooking slowly breaks down the tough meat fibers while providing moisture to meat that might otherwise be dry.

● Most ovens vary in temperature. If you do not already have an oven thermometer, buy one. If the temperature setting does not match the thermometer reading, adjust the timing of your recipes accordingly. Keep a record of your adjustments; it will be helpful in achieving consistency in the proper cooking of your dishes.

● The one item I cannot live without is an inexpensive 4-inch wire cake tester, which I use for testing game birds. I stick it into the bird's breast to check the color of the juices—they will run clear if the bird is done—and it leaves the breast unmarred.

Recipes

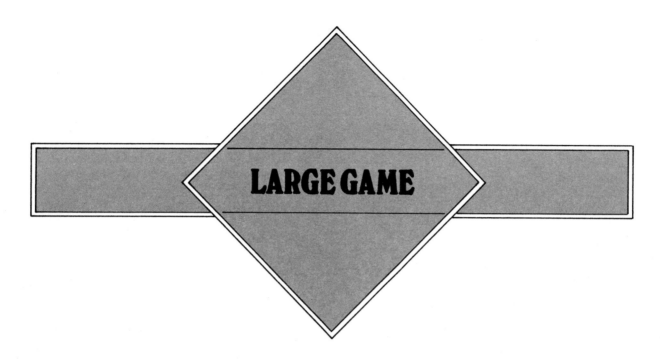

LARGE GAME

The word "venison" refers to the flesh of mammals from the family Cervidae. This family, which includes most of the common North American large game animals, such as the moose, elk, mule deer, black-tailed deer and white-tailed deer, is classified by the even-toed cloven hooves of its members. The males grow branched antlers every year which they shed after the mating season.

Venison is an especially lean meat, containing approximately 2 percent fat, while beef, depending on the cut of meat, contains 5 to 14 percent fat. This lack of fat in venison makes certain cooking methods advisable.

Stew meat can be either browned first to seal in the juices and then baked with the addition of liquid, or it can be put directly into a cooking liquid and baked at a low temperature. The first method will give you flavorful meat and the second method will give you a fine rich sauce.

My favorite way of cooking venison steaks is to coat the meat in seasoned flour and sauté it quickly so that it is medium-rare inside. Sprinkled with salt and freshly ground pepper, nothing could be more delicious. If you eat venison only once a year, this is the method I recommend. However, there are many of us who have freezers filled to capacity with wild game. As with any type of food, cooking it by the same method over and over again becomes routine. The recipes that follow are guides to assist you in new adventures in venison cooking. Use your own imagination and creativity to adjust the recipes to your taste.

Sautéed Venison with Green Pasta

Green pasta, generally made with spinach, is a delicious and colorful accompaniment to venison. If you do not want to make your own pasta and are unable to buy it fresh, use an imported brand made with all semolina, a hard durum wheat flour. This gives the pasta an excellent, firm texture.

1-pound, 12-ounce can Italian plum tomatoes with juice
3 cloves garlic
5 tablespoons butter
½ teaspoon salt
¼ teaspoon pepper
1½ pounds venison steak
⅓ cup flour
2 teaspoons paprika
½ pound fresh mushrooms, cleaned and sliced
4 tablespoons butter
1½ tablespoons safflower oil
1 pound green pasta
Freshly grated Parmesan cheese

Puree the tomatoes and their juice with the garlic in a blender or food processor. If you wish a seedless sauce, run the mixture through a food mill. Place the puree in a saucepan, add 1 tablespoon of the butter, the salt and pepper. Cook gently for 15 minutes, or until the sauce thickens.

Cut the meat across the grain into 2-by-¼-inch slices. Mix together the flour and paprika and roll each piece of meat in the mixture.

Heat 2 tablespoons of the butter and sauté the mushrooms for 4 or 5 minutes. Season with salt and pepper and set aside on a warm plate.

Heat the oil until very hot and quickly sauté the venison, about 3 or 4 minutes.

Meanwhile, cook and drain the pasta. Add the mushrooms and the remaining butter, toss and turn into a warm shallow bowl. Gently pile the meat on the pasta mixture in the center of the bowl. Pour the hot tomato sauce over the meat and mushrooms and serve immediately with freshly grated Parmesan cheese.

When Jefferson dispatched the explorers Meriwether Lewis and William Clark to pioneer the overland route westward up the Missouri and down the Columbia rivers, both captains kept daily journals. Clark recorded in his one December day that Lewis had not returned and "a 1000 conjectures had crowded into my mind respecting his probable situation and safety." Later that day, however, the captain returned with his men "haveing found a good situation and elk sufficient to winter on, his party killed 6 elk and 5 deer in their absence."

Bill's Venison Tortillas

Of all the recipes in this book, this one in particular is our family favorite. It is very filling and needs only a small tossed green salad and a glass or two of good beer to round out the meal.

MARINADE:
½ teaspoon crushed oregano
½ cup beef stock
   (see page 82)
½ cup safflower oil
2 cloves garlic, crushed
¼ teaspoon ground cumin

1 pound venison steak
3 tablespoons butter or vegetable
   oil (optional)
12 6-inch flour tortillas
2 cups refried beans
1 ripe avocado, peeled, pitted and
   pureed with ½ teaspoon lemon
   juice and 1 clove garlic
2 cups sour cream
1 teaspoon ground cumin
Fresh cilantro, for garnish
Salsa, to taste

Additional garnishes:
   Shredded lettuce
   Chopped tomatoes
   Chopped black olives
   Chopped green onions
   Grated cheddar cheese

Blend the marinade ingredients together and marinate the venison in the mixture for at least 30 minutes.

Place the tortillas in a damp cloth in a warm oven for 15 minutes. Warm the refried beans either in the oven or on the stove for 10 minutes. Blend the rest of the cumin into the sour cream. Remove the meat from the marinade and barbecue over a moderately hot fire until medium-rare, or sauté it quickly in 3 tablespoons of butter or oil. Slice the meat across the grain into ¼-inch-by-2¼-inch strips.

To assemble: Place a tortilla in the palm of your hand. Spread a layer of beans down the center of the tortilla, followed by the meat, avocado, sour cream, salsa and a few sprigs of fresh cilantro. Add additional garnishes, if desired. Roll up lengthwise and serve as finger food.

Although we traditionally think of American Indians as hunters armed with bow and arrow, the pre-European occupants of this country used quite an array of techniques for catching and preparing game. In addition to hunting with weapons such as bow and arrow, lances, blowguns, and slings, there were the more passive methods of digging pits and setting traps with nooses and nets. They cooked their food by the same three basic methods we use: broiling, roasting or boiling. Their ovens were earth ovens, similar to those still used for luaus in Hawaii. A hole would be dug in the ground and filled with hot stones from the fire; then the meat would be wrapped in leaves, placed in the oven and covered over with dirt until cooked.

Venison Chili

Serves 8

Venison makes excellent chili, especially when cooked with flavorful dried pinto beans. Serve this with a crisp green salad and homemade cornbread.

1 pound dried pinto beans, soaked
   overnight in water to cover
2 pounds venison
3 cloves garlic
1 large onion, chopped
6-ounce can tomato sauce
1½ teaspoons salt
1 tablespoon chili powder

Cook the beans in water for 45 minutes to 1 hour, or until tender.

Grind the venison and garlic together in a food processor or through the 3/16-inch blade of a meat grinder.

Combine the beans, onion, tomato sauce, salt and chili powder in a large saucepan and cook over moderate heat, stirring from time to time, until the mixture thickens, about 2 to 3 hours.

VARIATION: For an unusual and delicious tortilla filling, cook down any leftover chili until very thick. Stuff into flour tortillas and top with sour cream and guacamole.

Venison Stroganoff

This mouth-watering combination of sautéed venison, garlic, onions and mushrooms smothered in a rich sour cream sauce derives its name from Count Paul Stroganoff, a 19th-century Russian diplomat. Unlike most Stroganoff recipes, the meat in this recipe is cooked for a very short time, which allows the venison to retain its natural juices.

1 clove garlic, crushed
1 large onion, finely chopped
7 tablespoons butter
½ pound fresh mushrooms
Salt and pepper, to taste
1½ pounds venison steak, cut into
  3-by-½-inch strips
1 cup beef stock (see page 82)
1 cup sour cream
3 cups hot buttered noodles or
  long-grain rice
Paprika
Few sprigs fresh parsley

Gently sauté the garlic and onions in 3 tablespoons of the butter for 15 minutes, or until tender.

Add 3 more tablespoons of butter to the pan and sauté the mushrooms for 3 to 5 minutes. Add salt and pepper to taste, then transfer the mushroom mixture to a bowl and set aside.

Lightly flour the meat strips, then add the last tablespoon of butter to the skillet, heat until hot, and brown the floured meat strips. Add the beef broth and cook for 3 to 5 minutes. Add the mushroom-onion mixture and the sour cream and heat gently.

Serve over hot buttered noodles or long-grain rice. Sprinkle with paprika and a few sprigs of fresh parsley.

Big Game Hash

This hearty combination of ground venison, onions and potatoes makes a substantial meal that is well rounded out by a crisp spinach salad and a loaf of oatmeal bread served with sweet cream butter. If you wish, you can serve a sauce such as Hunter's Brown Sauce (page 83) or Horseradish and Sour Cream Sauce (page 26), on the side.

1 pound round steak,
  finely ground
½ cup finely chopped onion
1 cup grated potato
½ teaspoon salt
3 tablespoons safflower oil
Freshly ground pepper
Pinch of red pepper

Combine all the ingredients and shape into patties. Heat the oil in a skillet until moderately hot and fry the patties about 8 to 10 minutes, until they are thoroughly cooked and nicely browned on both sides.

Serve plain or with one of the sauces suggested above.

Grilled Venison Steaks with Garlic and Vermouth

Venison, being low in fat, needs to kept moist during cooking, particularly grilling. I usually wrap bacon strips around the steaks or brush them with about 4 tablespoons melted butter or bacon fat. Serve them with Horseradish and Sour Cream Sauce (below) on the side.

4 venison steaks
4 strips bacon
2 cloves garlic, peeled and cut in half
1 tablespoon dry vermouth
Salt and freshly ground pepper

Rub each piece of meat thoroughly with a half clove of garlic. Wrap each steak with a strip of bacon and secure with a toothpick. Grill for 3 to 5 minutes on each side, over a moderately hot fire. Transfer to a warm platter, sprinkle with vermouth, salt and freshly ground pepper, and serve.

HORSERADISH AND SOUR CREAM SAUCE

Makes 1 cup

This simple sauce keeps well for up to a week if refrigerated.

1 cup sour cream
2 teaspoons hot prepared horseradish

Mix together the sour cream and horseradish and serve with dark game meat.

Barbecued Backstrap

Serves 3-4

Nestling along the backbone, the backstrap is the most tender, and therefore most prized cut of venison. The following method of preparing it, marinated in a Chinese-inspired sauce and then barbecued, is especially good. Serve it with a cold Chinese noodle salad and tender spears of fresh asparagus. The backstrap is also good served with Hunter's Brown Sauce (page 83).

1 clove garlic, crushed
2 tablespoons soy sauce
3 tablespoons hoisin sauce
1 tablespoon honey
1½ pounds strip venison backstrap
3 strips bacon

Combine the garlic, soy sauce, hoisin sauce and honey. Rub the mixture generously into the meat and let it marinate for 5 to 6 hours. Wrap the bacon strips around the middle and ends of the meat and secure with toothpicks.

Barbecue the meat for 9 minutes on each side over a very hot fire.

Venison Steak with Cracked Pepper

Serves 4

Venison steak covered with freshly cracked pepper and a light brandy sauce is truly delicious. The secret of keeping the meat juicy is to sear the meat quickly in order to seal it. Horseradish and Sour Cream Sauce (opposite) or Hunter's Brown Sauce (page 83) are also good accompaniments.

2 pounds venison round steak
¼ cup brandy
2 tablespoons butter or
   safflower oil
Salt
Freshly cracked pepper
Chopped fresh parsley,
   for garnish

Pat the meat dry, rub it with butter or oil and a generous coating of freshly cracked pepper. Let it sit at room temperature for at least an hour.

Heat a large skillet over moderately high heat and add the oil. Place the meat in the pan and cook for about 2 minutes, or until the juices begin accumulating on the top. Turn, and cook for another 2 minutes. Do not turn again. Transfer the meat to a warm platter.

Scrape the bottom of the pan to collect all of the cooking juices and add the brandy. Cook over high heat 1 to 2 minutes, then add the salt and more pepper, if necessary. Pour over the meat.

Garnish the steak with chopped parsley and serve immediately.

Venison Mincemeat

This excellent and simple mincemeat is not quite traditional. Most mincemeat recipes call for suet, but I prefer butter. My version, which makes enough for about three pies, freezes well. To make an unusual mincemeat pie, bake the pie in a springform pan and remove the pan when the pie has cooled. Serve with Scotch Butter Sauce (recipe follows).

MINCEMEAT:
8 tablespoons butter
2 pounds venison scraps, finely
   chopped
10 Golden Delicious apples,
   peeled, cored and coarsely
   chopped
2 pounds raisins
2 cups raw brown sugar
2 teaspoons cinnamon
1 teaspoon freshly grated nutmeg
1 teaspoon ground cloves
1 teaspoon allspice
1½ teaspoons salt
¼ cup grated orange rind
   (optional)
Apple cider to cover
1 cup brandy (optional)

Heat the butter in a large 6-quart pot. Add the remaining mincemeat ingredients and cook slowly until the apples and raisins are soft, about 1½ hours. Cool, add the brandy and set aside 8 cups of the mixture to fill the pie shell. Ladle the remainder into freezer containers, label and freeze.

VENISON MINCEMEAT PIE

Makes a 10-inch double-crust pie

PIE PASTRY:
3 cups flour
½ teaspoon salt
8 tablespoons chilled butter, cut into small pieces
8 tablespoons chilled shortening
6-8 tablespoons ice water

8 cups venison mincemeat (see opposite page)
2 tablespoons heavy cream

To make the pastry, place the flour and salt in a deep bowl. Cut the butter and shortening into the flour until the mixture resembles coarse meal. Sprinkle the water over the mixture, tossing it with a fork. Form the pastry into a ball, place it in a plastic bag and chill for at least an hour.

Or, place the flour, salt and butter in a food processor. Flick the pulse button on and off about 10 times, or until the mixture resembles small peas. Turn the machine on and gradually add the ice water, processing until the mixture begins to form a ball. Form the pastry into a disk and chill as directed above.

When you are ready to make the pie, preheat the oven to 375 degrees.

Roll out half of the pastry on a floured board to fit a 10-inch springform pan. Place the pastry in the pan, pressing it gently against the sides and bottom of the pan. Evenly distribute 8 cups of the mincemeat in the pastry.

Roll out the remaining half of the pastry to fit the top of the pan and place it over the mincemeat. Trim off the edge of the crust. Cut a 1-inch hole in the center of the pie with a pastry cutter or a sharp knife. Brush the top of the pie with the cream.

Bake the pie in the preheated oven for 40 minutes, or until the crust is golden brown. Serve warm with Scotch Butter Sauce (below).

SCOTCH BUTTER SAUCE

Makes 1½ cups

This sauce can be made three to four days ahead of time and stored in a covered container in the refrigerator.

8 tablespoons butter
⅓ cup cream
3 cups confectioners' sugar
3 tablespoons Scotch whisky

Heat the butter in a saucepan. Stir in the cream, sugar and whisky and beat until the mixture is smooth and has a creamy consistency. Serve 2 to 3 tablespoons of the sauce, warmed, if desired, over pieces of freshly baked mincemeat pie.

SMALL GAME

Americans have been hunting small game since well before the first Pilgrims stepped off the *Mayflower*. These small animals not only saved many settlers from starvation, but also kept them warm with their furry pelts. This chapter concentrates on one member of the family Leporidae, the cottontail rabbit, which is the most popular small game animal eaten by hunters in the United States today. It is widely distributed throughout North America, and because it reproduces rapidly, it is seldom in short supply.

The cottontail rabbit runs for a living, which means that its flesh is fairly free of fat. A hundred grams of rabbit meat contains 5 percent fat, almost the same amount as pheasant. This low fat content means that rabbit should be cooked in a liquid or with a fat such as bacon and served with a sauce. Fruit sauces are particularly well suited to rabbit.

Broiled Tarragon Rabbit
with Herb Mayonnaise

Serves 4

This dish is a good one to serve in hot weather. Cook the rabbit ahead of time and let it cool completely. Serve it on a decorative platter along with the herb mayonnaise, a cold rice salad and ears of freshly grilled corn.

**2½-pound rabbit, cut into
    serving pieces
½ cup safflower oil
½ cup olive oil
½ teaspoon whole tarragon,
    crushed
½ teaspoon salt
¼ teaspoon pepper**

**HERB MAYONNAISE:
1 egg yolk
1 teaspoon red wine vinegar
½ teaspoon salt
¾ cup olive oil
¾ cup safflower oil
3 tablespoons chopped scallions
3 tablespoons chopped parsley
1 clove garlic, finely chopped**

Place the rabbit in a 9-by-13-inch pan. Combine the safflower oil, olive oil, salt and pepper and pour it over the rabbit. Marinate in a cool place for 4 hours, turning the pieces every half hour.

Preheat the broiler.

Place the rabbit pieces in a broiling pan and cook under the preheated broiler for 10 minutes. Turn the meat and brush generously with the marinade. Broil another 8 to 10 minutes, until deep golden brown. Cool and chill the rabbit.

To make the herb mayonnaise, place the egg yolk, vinegar, salt, scallions, parsley and garlic in the bowl of a food processor or blender. Process for 30 seconds, and with the machine still running, add the oils in a slow, steady stream.

Arrange the chilled rabbit on a platter and spread a heaping tablespoon of herb mayonnaise on each piece. Serve immediately.

Grilled Rabbit with Rosemary and Lime Butter

Serves 4

Rabbit grilled over mesquite charcoal has a wonderful savory flavor and a moist texture. This is because mesquite burns very intensely and therefore quickly sears the meat so that none of the juices escape.

2½ pound rabbit, cut into serving
   pieces
2 cloves garlic, finely chopped
1 teaspoon rosemary
½ teaspoon cracked pepper
½ cup olive oil
8 tablespoons butter
½ cup fresh lime juice
4 slices lime, for garnish

Rub the rabbit pieces with the garlic. Place them in a 9-by-13-inch pan and sprinkle them with the rosemary and pepper. Pour the oil over the rabbit pieces and marinate for 4 hours, turning the pieces every half hour.

Grill the rabbit over mesquite charcoal for 30 minutes, or until the juices run clear.

Meanwhile, melt the butter in a small saucepan and stir in the lime juice. Place the cooked rabbit on a warm platter and brush it generously with the butter mixture. Garnish with fresh lime slices and serve immediately.

Mustard Rabbit Baked in Rock Salt

Serves 4

This method of preparing rabbit, wrapped in spinach leaves and baked on salt, produces delightfully flavorful, moist meat. To serve, discard the salty outer spinach leaves. The inner leaves should remain covering the rabbit, as they not only add flavor, but make an attractive presentation. Serve this dish with Madeira Sauce (page 83), if desired.

1½-pound rabbit, cut up
4 tablespoons Dijon-style mustard
1 teaspoon tarragon, crushed
1 clove garlic, crushed
1 pound fresh spinach, cleaned
1 box rock salt

Preheat the oven to 400 degrees.

Rinse the rabbit and pat dry with paper towels. Mix together the mustard, tarragon and garlic and rub the mixture generously over the rabbit pieces.

Wrap each rabbit piece in two layers of spinach leaves, making sure to cover all parts of the flesh. Secure the leaves in place with twine.

Pour ½ inch of rock salt into a deep baking dish. Place the rabbit pieces on top of the salt. Pour another ½ inch of salt over the rabbit. Bake in the preheated oven for 40 minutes.

To serve, discard the salty outer spinach leaves and twine. Arrange the rabbit on a warm platter and serve immediately.

Curried Rabbit with Chutney

Serves 4

I like to use mild curry powder in this dish, so that the delicate flavor of the rabbit comes through. Serve it over rice cooked in chicken stock and lightly flavored with saffron.

2½-pound rabbit, cut into serving
    pieces
½ cup all-purpose flour
3 tablespoons safflower oil
1 cup heavy cream
¼ cup golden grapes (optional)
3 tablespoons mango chutney
½ teaspoon salt
¼ teaspoon white pepper
2 teaspoons curry powder

Dredge the rabbit pieces in the flour. Heat the oil in a skillet and add the rabbit. Cook for 10 minutes, turning often, until golden brown.

Mix the remaining ingredients together and pour them over the rabbit. Cover with a tight-fitting lid and simmer for 20 more minutes, or until the juices of the rabbit run clear. Remove the meat to a warm plate and cover to keep warm.

Reduce the sauce over high heat until it thickens and turns deep brown. Pour it over the rabbit and serve immediately.

Rabbit with Prunes in Pinot Noir

Serves 4

This combination may seem unusual, but the prunes, wine and seasonings of this dish cook down to an exceptionally delicious sauce.

1½ cups large pitted prunes,
    halved
3 cups Pinot Noir
2½-pound rabbit, cut into serving
    pieces
1 cup beef stock (see page 82)
2 tablespoons red wine vinegar
2 shallots, minced
3 sprigs fresh thyme, or
    ½ teaspoon dried
½ teaspoon salt
¼ teaspoon white pepper

Marinate the prunes in the wine for 1 hour.

Place the rabbit in a deep nonaluminum skillet. Add the prunes, wine and remaining ingredients. Cover and simmer for about an hour, or until the juices of the rabbit run clear.

Remove the rabbit pieces to a warm plate and cover to keep warm. Boil the sauce over high heat until reduced by half and slightly thickened. Adjust the seasoning, if necessary, pour over the rabbit and serve immediately.

Braised Rabbit with Rosemary and Sour Cream

Serves 4

Braising is a good moist-heat method for cooking rabbit, and this recipe makes a fine, tasty sauce. This dish is also excellent made with pheasant in place of rabbit.

4 tablespoons butter
½ cup finely chopped onion
¾ teaspoon sugar
1½-2-pound rabbit, cut up
1 cup chicken stock (see page 82)
2 sprigs fresh parsley
¼ teaspoon whole rosemary, crushed
½ cup sour cream
Salt and freshly ground pepper, to taste
2 teaspoons cornstarch dissolved in ¼ cup water, if needed

Heat the butter in a heavy skillet. Add the onions and the sugar and sauté for about 8 minutes, until soft and golden brown. Add the rabbit pieces, chicken stock, chopped parsley and crushed rosemary. Cover the pan and simmer for 30 minutes, or until the juices of the rabbit run clear.

Transfer the rabbit to a serving platter and place in a warm oven.

Stir the sour cream into the cooking juices and, if necessary, thicken the sauce with 2 teaspoons of cornstarch dissolved in ¼ cup water. Pour over the rabbit and serve immediately on warm plates.

Rabbit Braised in Apples and Cream

Serves 4

Rabbit and fruit just naturally go well together, especially tart green apples. The rabbit in this dish is slowly braised in both apples and applejack, a brandy distilled from hard cider, as well as cream, producing a rich well-flavored sauce.

6 tablespoons butter
2 green apples, peeled, cored and cut into ¼-inch slices
1 cup chopped onions
2½-pound rabbit, cut into serving pieces
⅔ cup applejack
1 cup heavy cream
½ teaspoon salt
¼ teaspoon white pepper

Heat 3 tablespoons of the butter in a deep flameproof casserole over moderate heat. Add the apple slices and cook for 10 more minutes, or until the slices begin to soften. Remove them from the pan and set aside. Add 3 more tablespoons of butter to the casserole and cook the onions for 8 minutes, or until they begin to brown.

Add the rabbit pieces to the casserole and cook, turning often, until browned, about 10 minutes. Add the applejack and flame it. Gently stir in the cream, sautéed apple slices, salt and white pepper.

Cook the rabbit over moderate heat for 30 minutes. The rabbit is cooked when the juices run clear.

UPLAND GAME

I find that the excitement of upland game hunting carries over from the field to the kitchen. The many species of land-loving birds challenge the cook to bring out the best of the delicate yet distinctive flavor in their succulent meat; it is for good reason that many of these birds are the most prized game of all, sought by cooks the world over.

Recipes for many game birds are interchangeable. Pheasant, grouse and partridge are composed mostly of similarly flavored light meat.

Quail is also composed of light meat, but it is fairly tender and moist—more like chicken than other game birds. It can be cooked by any method you would use for chicken; just remember to reduce the cooking time.

Dove and pigeon, both dark-meated birds, share many recipes, too, although dove is usually the more tender of the two.

I like to marinate light-meated upland game birds, particularly partridge and pheasant, in an oil-based sauce. Because these birds have a very mild flavor, they are enhanced by well-seasoned sauces.

Pheasant Baked in Phyllo Pastry

According to legend, when Jason and the Argonauts brought the golden fleece back to Greece from Colchis, a country on the eastern shore of the Black Sea, they also brought with them beautifully colored birds from the banks of the Phasis river. Consequently, the scientific name for the ring-necked pheasant is Phasianus colchicus. *This dish is usually made with boned pheasant breasts, but I have also prepared it with half a whole pheasant. It tastes just as good, but is a little more difficult to eat. Serve this dish with the Madeira Sauce on page 83, if you wish.*

4 pheasant breasts, boned
Salt and freshly ground pepper, to taste
1 cup cooked short-grain brown rice
1 cup cooked wild rice
16 sheets phyllo dough, cut in half
8 tablespoons butter, melted

Preheat the oven to 375 degrees. Grease a baking sheet.

Pound the breasts lightly so that the meat is about ¼ inch thick. Rub the meat with salt and freshly ground pepper.

Combine the two kinds of rice in a bowl.

For each breast you will need 8 sheets of phyllo and ½ cup of the rice mixture. Lay one piece of phyllo down on a dry surface. Brush it completely with the melted butter. Continue layering and buttering until you have a stack of 8 buttered sheets. Lay a pheasant breast in the middle of each stack. Place ½ cup of the rice mixture on top of each piece of pheasant. Fold the bottom edge of each phyllo stack over the top of the filling, covering the rice completely. Fold both outside edges in over the phyllo. Roll each packet towards the top edge to seal in the filling. Brush the packets with butter, making sure the seam and outer edges are thoroughly glazed. Place each packet, seam side down, on a greased baking sheet and bake in the preheated oven for 45 minutes.

NOTE: If you wish, you can cut the pheasant into bite-sized pieces before filling the pastry. Reduce the cooking time by about 5 minutes.

The Audubon Society, founded in 1886, sprang from the anti-plumage movement of the middle 1800s, which protested the slaughter of birds to provide extravagant feather decorations for women's hats and clothing. The society's original goals were to prevent the killing of any wild birds not used for food, the destruction of nests or eggs of any wild bird, and the wearing of feathers as ornaments or trimmings for dress.

Pheasant with Mushrooms and Onions, Chasseur   *Serves 3-4*

Chasseur *means hunter or huntsman in French. This time-honored method of braising game with onions, wine, mushrooms and tomatoes remains a favorite way to prepare game when my family's hunters return home with their limit of game birds. Serve this dish over steaming brown rice.*

5 tablespoons butter
½ cup chopped onion
½ cup chopped mushrooms
½ cup flour
½ teaspoon salt
¼ teaspoon pepper
½ teaspoon oregano
1½-pound pheasant, cut up
2 tomatoes, peeled, seeded and
**   coarsely chopped**
1 cup chicken stock
½ cup dry white wine
¼ cup water
2 sprigs fresh parsley, finely
**   chopped**

Heat 2 tablespoons of the butter in a large heavy skillet. Add the onions and sauté until slightly brown, about 5 minutes. Add the mushrooms and a sprinkling of salt and pepper and cook for 3 more minutes or until the mushrooms begin to soften. Transfer the mixture to a plate and set aside.

Combine the flour, remaining salt, pepper and oregano. Set aside 1½ tablespoons of the mixture. Generously coat the pheasant pieces with the flour mixture.

Heat the remaining butter in the same skillet and add the pheasant. Gently brown the meat over moderate heat, turning the pieces to brown evenly. This should take about 8 to 10 minutes.

Add the onions, mushrooms, tomatoes, chicken broth and wine to the skillet. Cover with a tight-fitting lid and simmer for 30 minutes, or until the pheasant is tender. Mix the reserved flour mixture with ¼ cup water. Transfer the pheasant to a warm platter and add the flour mixture to the cooking juices, stirring constantly until the sauce thickens. Adjust the seasoning, if needed, and pour over the pheasant. Sprinkle with fresh parsley and serve immediately.

Clay Pot Pheasant with Mixed Vegetables

The sautéed vegetables in this dish form a base, called a mirepoix *in French, used to flavor meats, fish and shellfish, or as a base for soups and stews. I cut the vegetables into fairly large pieces so that they retain their shape under high heat. Pheasant cooked in the moist heat of a clay pot is amazingly succulent, and the juices that accumulate in the bottom of the pot, seasoned by the vegetables and meat, create a fine well-flavored sauce.*

2 tablespoons butter
1 small onion, sliced
1 large carrot, peeled and cut into
    2-by-½-inch sticks
1 large stalk celery, cut into
    2-by-½-inch sticks
½ teaspoon each dried rosemary,
    sage and thyme, mixed together
1½-pound pheasant, skinned and
    cleaned
Salt and pepper, to taste
6 slices bacon
4 thin slices prosciutto ham

STUFFING:
1 small carrot, peeled and cut into
    thirds
1 stalk celery, cut into thirds
1 small onion, peeled and cut into
    thirds
1 slice bacon

Soak a clay pot in cold water for 15 minutes.

Heat the butter in a frying pan and add the onion, carrot and celery and a pinch of the herb mixture. Sauté quickly for 5 minutes.

Pat the pheasant dry with paper towels. Place the rest of the herb mixture in the palm of your hand and crush gently to release the fragrant oils. Rub the crushed herbs generously over the bird and inside the cavity, along with a good sprinkling of salt and pepper.

Place the stuffing of carrot, celery, onion and bacon inside the pheasant. Tie the legs of the bird together.

Place the rest of the vegetables in the bottom of the clay pot. Set the bird on top of the vegetables and drape the pheasant with the slices of prosciutto. Place a layer of bacon over the prosciutto, completely covering the bird.

Put the lid on the pot and place in a cold oven. Turn the oven to 475 degrees and cook undisturbed for 50 minutes.

To serve, place the cooked pheasant on a warm platter and pour the vegetables and juices over the bird.

Sautéed Pheasant with Lemon

Serves 4

Pheasants, partridges and quail all belong to the order Phasianidae, which includes 189 species. All of them are hen-like, with sturdy legs for running and scrapping. Their bills are slightly curved, allowing them to feed on ground vegetation, insects and seeds. The pheasant we are familiar with, Phasianus colchicus, is often called ring-necked because of its distinctive band of white feathers around the neck. It is native to Asia, which is why it is also called Chinese pheasant.

I like to serve this dish with either Hollandaise (page 84) or Madeira Sauce (page 83). Green pasta sprinkled with Parmesan cheese and a green salad with Italian dressing complete the meal.

4 pheasant breasts, skinned
1 teaspoon salt
½ teaspoon freshly ground pepper
¼ cup olive oil
¼ cup safflower oil
3 tablespoons butter
Juice of ½ lemon
1 teaspoon capers (optional)
¼ cup parsley, finely chopped

Wipe the pheasant breasts dry with paper towels, then rub them with salt and pepper.

Place the pheasant breasts in a shallow bowl. Combine the olive and safflower oils and pour over the meat. Leave to marinate for 6 to 8 hours, turning every couple of hours.

Slice the meat into ¼-inch-thick slices. Heat the butter in a skillet until it bubbles, then sauté the meat for 4 to 5 minutes, turning once.

Pour the lemon juice over the pheasant and sprinkle with the parsley and capers, if desired. Serve immediately on warm plates.

Every group of birds has its special term, most of them dating from medieval days when hunting was carried on by hawks, released from their masters' gloved hands to fly in search of prey, swooping down upon smaller birds and rabbits to kill them in an instant. Everyone knows about a gaggle of geese; how about a paddling of ducks? Some others: a siege of herons, a bevy of quail, a congregation of plover, a fall of woodcock, a murmuration of starlings, a charm of goldfinches, a spring of teal, a muster of peacocks, a duel of turtle-doves, and an exaltation of larks.

Sautéed Partridge with Vegetables and Madeira

Serves 4-5

There are three main species of partridge found in North America: the red-legged partridge, the chukar partridge and the Hungarian partridge, and recipes for them are interchangeable.

The garlic-flavored breadcrumbs in this recipe help to seal in the juices of each bird and thicken the sauce. Serve this dish as a main course with freshly steamed artichokes, a loaf of crusty French bread, and a bottle of chilled Chardonnay.

4 tablespoons butter
1 carrot, peeled and cut into 2-inch lengths
1 small onion, peeled and cut into eighths
1 clove garlic, finely chopped
1 cup Italian-flavored breadcrumbs
2 1-pound partridges, cut into pieces
2 cups beef stock (see page 82)
2 teaspoons tomato paste
2 tablespoons Madeira
¼ pound mushrooms, sliced

Heat 2 tablespoons of the butter in a heavy skillet. Add the carrot and the onion and sauté for 10 minutes, or until the onion becomes quite brown. Transfer the vegetables to a dish and set aside. Melt 2 more tablespoons of the butter and brush it over the birds.

Combine the garlic and the breadcrumbs. Roll the partridge pieces in the breadcrumbs mixture and press the crumbs firmly onto the meat.

Put the carrot and onion back in the pan and carefully brown the breaded pieces of bird over moderately low heat, turning to brown all sides. This should take about 10 minutes.

Add the beef stock, tomato paste, Madeira and mushrooms and cook for 15 more minutes, or until the juices of the birds run clear. Serve immediately.

Chinese Chukars

Serves 2 as a main course, 4 as an appetizer

The chukar partridge, Alectoris chukar, *is distinguished from its oft-mistaken cousin, the red-legged partridge* (Alectoris rufa), *by its clearly delineated collar. Chukars marinated and sautéed are amazingly moist and flavorful. Serve them as a tasty appetizer or as a main course with gingered carrots and a green salad garnished with fresh orange slices.*

2 1-pound chukars, cut in half vertically
¼ cup safflower oil
¼ cup soy sauce
¼ cup brown sugar
3 tablespoons butter

Dry the birds, inside and out, with paper towels. Combine the oil, soy sauce and brown sugar. Pour the mixture over the chukars and rub into the flesh and cavity of each bird. Cover and leave to marinate in a cool place for 6 to 8 hours.

Heat the butter in a skillet and quickly sauté the birds over high heat. Cook 3 to 4 minutes per side, turning once. Serve immediately.

Chukars in Garlic Cream

Serves 3

Chukar partridges are found in dry steep canyons along riverbeds and can be distinguished from other birds by their "chuk ... chuk ... chuk" call. Serve these roasted birds as a main course with buttered fettuccine noodles and fresh tender peas.

2 1-pound chukars
1 teaspoon salt
½ teaspoon freshly ground pepper
4 slices day-old garlic bread, cubed
½ cup chicken stock (see page 82)
¼ cup dry white wine
2 cloves garlic, peeled and crushed
2 tablespoons butter
½ cup heavy cream
1½ teaspoons cornstarch
1 teaspoon cold water
4 sprigs fresh parsley

Preheat the oven to 350 degrees.

Dry the birds, inside and out, with paper towels. Rub a generous amount of salt and freshly ground pepper both on and in the birds. Stuff the cavities with the garlic bread.

Place the birds in a small casserole and add the chicken stock, wine, garlic and butter. Cover the dish and bake in the preheated oven for 40 to 45 minutes, or until the juices of the meat run clear. Remove the birds to a warm platter and cover with foil.

Stir the cream into the casserole juices. Dissolve the cornstarch in the teaspoon of cold water and gradually stir into the casserole juices. Stir constantly over low heat until the sauce has slightly thickened. Adjust the seasoning and pour over the birds.

Arrange the chukars on individual warm plates, garnish with the parsley and serve immediately.

Roast Partridge with Leeks and Sour Cream

Serves 2-3

The gray partridge is also called Bohemian partridge, English partridge, European partridge, Hungarian partridge, Hun and Hunkie. Ignoring the multitude of names, any member of the partridge, grouse or pheasant family can be used in this recipe.

    The leek is one of the mildest-tasting members of the onion family and its delicate flavor is a pleasing accompaniment to the rich meat of game birds. I like to bake this recipe in a gratin dish, and serve it directly from the dish at the dinner table.

1 pound partridge
½ teaspoon salt
½ teaspoon whole thyme, crushed
1 carrot, peeled and cut into
    2-by-½-inch sticks
½ pound leeks, cleaned and cut
    in half vertically
2 slices bacon
1 cup chicken stock (see page 82)
½ cup sour cream
2 teaspoons butter
Freshly ground pepper

Preheat the oven to 350 degrees.

Dry the bird, inside and out, with paper towels. Generously rub the salt and thyme into the flesh and cavity of the bird.

Place the carrots and leeks in a heavy casserole. Set the partridge, breast side up, on top of the vegetables and lay the bacon slices over the bird's breast. Pour the chicken stock into the casserole, cover, and cook for 45 minutes, or until the juices of the partridge run clear.

Transfer the bird and vegetables to a warm platter and cover with foil. Stir the sour cream and butter into the pan juices and heat gently. Season the sauce with salt and freshly ground pepper.

Ladle half of the sauce over the bird and pour the rest into a warm gravy boat. Serve immediately.

Doves Baked in Horseradish Mask

Serves 4

Dove and pigeon, found throughout North America, are members of the same family (Columbidae) and can be cooked in the same ways. The young of both are known as squab and are about the size of large robins, weighing about 3 or 4 ounces each.

In this recipe, the birds are cooked in a mask, or covering, of horseradish, both as a flavoring and to protect the tender meat from the intense heat of the broiler. I like to serve them with a fresh fruit salad, grated raw carrots in a vinaigrette sauce and a loaf of freshly baked whole-wheat bread.

16-18 squab, plucked and cleaned
½ cup prepared horseradish
2 tablespoons brown sugar
¼ teaspoon salt

Preheat the oven to 400 degrees.

Dry the birds, inside and out, with paper towels and rub the cavities with salt. Place in a large baking dish.

Combine the horseradish and brown sugar into a paste, and coat each bird with the mixture.

Bake for 10 to 12 minutes, then turn the oven to broil and cook an additional 5 minutes, or until the mask is slightly browned.

Pigeons Baked in Bacon

Serves 4

Pigeons have dense and flavorful dark meat that goes particularly well with bacon. Serve these birds on toast that has been cut diagonally in half into triangles.

8 pigeons
1 teaspoon salt
½ teaspoon freshly ground pepper
2 tablespoons butter
8 slices bacon
8 toothpicks

Preheat the oven to 400 degrees.

Wipe each bird dry with paper towels and sprinkle with the salt and pepper inside and out.

Heat the butter and brush 1 tablespoon of it onto the birds. Wrap a piece of bacon around each bird and secure with a toothpick.

Pour the remaining butter into a baking dish and place the birds in the dish so that none of them are touching. Bake for 12 to 15 minutes, or until they are deep brown and the juices run clear.

Quail with Madeira

The light meat of quail has a fine flavor that needs little to enhance it. Serve these birds and their tasty sauce on a bed of mixed brown and wild rice, accompanied by fresh chanterelles (if you're lucky enough to come across them) that have been cooked in cream, and a green salad with walnuts.

4 quail, ready for cooking
Salt and pepper, to taste
4 cherry tomatoes
2 scallions, quartered
4 sprigs parsley
¼ cup flour
4 tablespoons butter
4 tablespoons brandy
4 tablespoons Madeira
1 teaspoon chives

Wipe the birds dry, inside and out, with paper towels. Season the cavities with salt and pepper and place a cherry tomato, 2 pieces of scallion and a sprig of fresh parsley inside each bird. Tie the legs together with string. Dredge each bird with flour.

Heat 2 tablespoons of the butter in a frying pan and sauté the birds over moderate heat, turning them every few minutes, until the juices of the meat run clear, about 15 minutes.

Remove the birds to a warm platter and add the brandy, Madeira, chives and remaining butter to the pan juices. Cook over high heat for 2 more minutes. Season with salt and pepper and pour the sauce over the birds.

Serve immediately.

Broiled Quail with Lemon Butter

Serves 4

This method of cooking quail is simple, quick and delicious. Serve the birds on toast points and garnish each plate with a sprig of fresh parsley and a slice of fresh lemon. Allow two to four quail per person.

12 quail, ready for cooking
4 tablespoons butter
Juice of ½ lemon
½ teaspoon dry mustard
1 tablespoon Dijon-style mustard
½ teaspoon crushed rosemary
**4 pieces freshly made toast,
  buttered and cut into triangles**

Preheat the broiler.

Dry the birds, inside and out, with paper towels and place them on a broiling pan, breast side up. Heat the butter in a skillet, and stir in the lemon juice, mustards and rosemary.

Broil the birds 4 to 6 inches from the heat for 10 to 12 minutes, brushing with the butter mixture generously every 3 to 4 minutes.

Place the cooked birds on the toast points and brush with the butter mixture once again. Serve immediately.

Baked Squab with Tomatoes

Serves 3-4

In France, this dish might be called Pigeonneau à la Provençale, *referring to the combination of tomatoes, garlic and olive oil so characteristic of the cooking of Provence in the south. The flavorful sauce is excellent for baking the robust dark meat of the squab.*

8 squab, ready for cooking
¼ cup olive oil
**Salt and freshly ground pepper,
  to taste**
8 medium-size tomatoes, halved
4 cloves garlic, crushed
4 sprigs parsley, chopped
½ cup breadcrumbs
**½ cup freshly grated Parmesan
  cheese**

Preheat the oven to 400 degrees.

Dry the birds, inside and out, with paper towels. Rub the birds thoroughly with a generous amount of the olive oil, then season with salt and pepper.

Seed each tomato half and place them, cut side up, in a shallow baking dish. Arrange the birds on the tomato shells.

Combine the garlic, parsley, breadcrumbs and Parmesan cheese. Spread the mixture evenly over the birds and tomatoes. Bake for 20 minutes.

Serve immediately on warm plates.

Stir-Fried Squab with Fresh Ginger

*Serves 2 as a main course,
4 as an appetizer*

This dish can be served either as an appetizer, with lots of napkins, or as a main course. If you offer it as a main course, serve it over rice and count at least two to three squab per person. These birds go particularly well served as an appetizer for Venison Steak with Cracked Pepper (see page 27).

½ teaspoon sesame oil
1½ tablespoons soy sauce
1 tablespoon dry sherry
2 teaspoon safflower oil
4 squab, cleaned and cut into quarters
½ cup red bell pepper, seeded and sliced into strips
½-inch piece fresh ginger, peeled and sliced
1 clove garlic, crushed

Mix together the sesame oil, soy sauce and sherry and set aside.

Heat the safflower oil in a wok or frying pan over moderately high heat until very hot. Add the squab, red pepper and ginger and cook, stirring constantly, for 2 minutes. Pour the sesame oil mixture over the squab and red peppers. Cook for 2 more minutes, stirring constantly.

Add the crushed garlic and toss thoroughly. Cook for 20 more seconds and serve immediately.

Broiled Squab

Serves 4

These delicious birds are very small, so be careful not to overcook them. I like to serve them with Madeira Sauce (page 83), braised Red Cabbage with Apples (see page 80) and potato pancakes.

12 squab, ready for cooking
4 tablespoons butter, melted
1 teaspoon paprika
1½ teaspoons salt
½ teaspoon freshly ground pepper

Preheat the broiler.

Split the squab down the backbone with poultry shears. Place the birds on a flat surface, breast side up, and firmly push down on the breastbones to flatten them slightly. Arrange the squab in a large broiling pan.

Brush the birds with the melted butter. Sprinkle them with the paprika, salt and freshly ground pepper.

Broil the squab for 8 to 9 minutes, turning them once during cooking.

Serve immediately on warm plates.

Squab Baked in Apple Cases

This recipe requires a little time to carve the apple cases. The effort is well worth it, though, for the result is impressive both in taste and presentation when it arrives at the dinner table.

12 squab, ready for cooking
1½ teaspoons salt
1½ teaspoons freshly ground
  pepper
6 large firm tart apples, peeled
  and cored (Gravenstein or
  Granny Smith, if possible)
¾ cup raisins
½ cup brandy
1 cup sour cream

Dry the birds, inside and out, with paper towels. Rub them well with salt and pepper.

Take the peeled and cored apples and stand them upright on a cutting board, stem end up. Hold the knife parallel to the cutting board and cut each apple in half. Slice a small piece off the end of each half if necessary, so that the half can sit flat. Scoop out each apple half to make a case to fit a bird. (Each whole apple, in effect, will hold 2 squab.)

Place the raisins and apple cases in a flameproof shallow baking dish. Pour the brandy over all and marinate for 1 hour at room temperature. Spoon the brandy over the apples frequently, soaking all parts.

Preheat the oven to 425 degrees.

Stuff 2 teaspoons of the marinated raisins inside each bird and place a bird inside each apple case in the dish. Reserve the brandy.

Bake the birds for 20 minutes in the preheated oven, then transfer them to a warm platter. Pour off all the grease that has accumulated in the dish. Place the dish on a burner over low heat, add the reserved brandy, and cook briefly, scraping the dish meanwhile to release the flavorful particles sticking to the bottom and sides. If you wish a perfectly smooth sauce, strain the brandy into a small bowl, then return it to the original dish. Stir in the sour cream and heat gently until very hot. Remove from the heat, season with salt if necessary, and pour the sauce over the birds.

Serve immediately on warm plates.

WATERFOWL

There is an old saying that the two greatest fools in the world are marathon runners and duck hunters. I am not sure whose mate started this rumor, but there may be some truth in it—certainly both these occupations take up an awful lot of time, and sitting for hours in a duck blind in freezing temperatures is not my notion of fun, although I don't complain. Few things are more succulent than roast wild duck, and I don't want to cut off my supplies.

One of the most common complaints I hear about wild birds is that they are dry and tough. I wonder how many people realize that *all* birds will be dry and tough if they are overcooked, even chicken and turkey.

First, you must understand that there are two theories of duck cookery. One is to cook the birds at a very high temperature for a short time. The other is to cook them at a moderately low temperature for a long time. I prefer the high-temperature method, but whichever method suits you, the secret of success lies hidden deep in the juices of the duck breast. Toward the end of cooking time, prick the breast with a fork or cake tester. For a medium-rare bird, the juices should run rose-color. A well-done bird's juices will be clear yellow. If no juices appear, you have overcooked the duck and the meat will be dry. Areas where shot has entered invariably produce red juices because of the blood that has gathered there, so I always check both breasts.

When cooking large and small birds together, always give the larger birds a 5- to 10-minute head start. For instance, mallards should be put in the oven at least 10 minutes ahead of the small teal.

I have found when entertaining that, sexist as it sounds, most men can eat a whole mallard while women generally do better with two teal. Everyone will need at least two napkins and a steak knife, and they will probably want plenty of freshly ground pepper. At the end of the evening you might remind everyone present to be thankful that they know some people crazy enough to spend their spare time duck hunting!

Widgeon Roasted in Foil

Serves 2

The American widgeon is also called the baldpate, because of its grayish head with a central white crown. When these birds are shot inland they have a delicious flavor, and I like to prepare them using this uncomplicated method.

2 widgeon, ready for cooking
½ teaspoon salt
½ teaspoon whole thyme
1 apple, cored and quartered
1 onion, peeled and quartered
2 stalks celery

Preheat the oven to 475 degrees.

Wipe the birds inside and out with a damp paper towel. Rub the cavities with equal portions of salt and thyme. Place 2 apple quarters, 2 onion quarters and a stalk of celery in each bird.

Wrap the birds individually in foil and bake in the preheated oven for 20 minutes. Open the foil around the breasts and broil for 5 to 10 minutes, or until the skin is crisp and brown.

Baked Mallard Stuffed with Brandied Apple and Onion

Serves 4

This is my favorite method for preparing duck, because it is simple and delicious. The apple and onion slices can be marinated in the brandy the night before, leaving little preparation when you are ready to cook.

2 apples, unpeeled, but cored
   and quartered
2 onions, quartered
½ cup brandy
4 mallards, ready for cooking,
   and at room temperature
½ teaspoon salt
½ teaspoon thyme
4 teaspoons butter
2 cups beef stock (see page 82)
Salt and pepper to taste

Soak the apples and onions in the brandy for at least an hour or overnight.

Preheat the oven to 475 degrees.

Wipe the mallards inside and out with a damp paper towel. Rub the cavities with equal parts of salt and thyme and stuff with the apple and onion slices, reserving the brandy. Rub the skin of the duck with the butter.

Bake in the preheated oven for 25 to 27 minutes, or until the juices run rose-color for a medium-rare bird, clear yellow for a well-done bird. Broil for 3 to 5 minutes more to crisp the skin. Transfer the ducks to a platter and place in a warm oven.

Degrease the pan juices, add the beef stock and boil the liquid to reduce it by half, stirring constantly to deglaze the caramelized bits. Add the reserved brandy and season with salt and pepper to taste. Strain, if necessary, and serve the sauce separately.

Sweet-and-Sour Duck Breasts

Serves 4

The unusual ingredients in this recipe are adaptations from a favorite country-style sparerib recipe. While the duck breasts are baking, a wonderful sweet-and-sour aroma with hints of garlic fills the air. Serve the breasts over freshly cooked and drained Chinese noodles.

6-8 duck breasts
2 4¾-ounce jars strained peaches
½ cup packed brown sugar
½ cup soy sauce
⅓ cup red wine vinegar
2 teaspoons ground ginger
2 cloves garlic, crushed
½ teaspoon salt
Pepper, to taste

Preheat the oven to 350 degrees.

Place the duck breasts in a heavy casserole.

Combine the remaining ingredients and pour over the breasts.

Cover, and bake in the preheated oven for 45 to 50 minutes, until the juices run rose-color for medium-rare and clear yellow for well-done.

Barbecued Duck in Honey

This recipe uses my favorite summer barbecue sauce. The orange juice and dry mustard give the duck a tangy, refreshing taste.

MARINADE:
⅓ cup butter
1 cup orange juice
½ cup honey
3 tablespoons soy sauce
3 tablespoons chopped parsley
2 tablespoons lemon juice
1 tablespoon dry mustard

1 whole orange, peeled and sliced
    crosswise
2 mallards, split in half
    lengthwise

Heat the butter in a saucepan and stir in the remaining marinade ingredients. Heat slowly over low heat for 3 to 5 minutes. Place the ducks in a 9-by-13-inch glass dish and pour over the marinade. Add the sliced orange. Marinate for 1 to 2 hours at room temperature, turning the ducks every 15 to 20 minutes.

Barbecue over a moderately hot fire, turning frequently to prevent burning, for 1 hour, or until the juices of the breasts run clear.

Mark Twain toured Europe in 1878 and subsequently wrote A Tramp Abroad. *In this work, he reviewed the sorts of European cuisine which did not appeal to his American taste. "There is here and there an American who will say he can remember rising from a European table d'hôte perfectly satisfied," he wrote, "but we must not overlook the fact that there is also here and there an American who will lie." In* A Tramp Abroad *he listed more than 60 American dishes which he was looking forward to having when he returned home. Among them were roast wild turkey, canvas-back duck, prairie hens, Missouri partridges, opossum and raccoon.*

In 1937 a private organization called Ducks Unlimited was formed. This group of waterfowl enthusiasts is still active today and over the years has raised more than $200 million for wildlife conservation.

Portland Pressed Duck

You do not have to travel to Paris and dine at the Tour d'Argent to eat pressed duck. This dish can be prepared in your own home, if you can find a duck press. Few of us are fortunate enough to own one, but check with friends, or inquire at your local gourmet shop, as many rent them out. Pressed duck is actually quite easy to make, and the extra effort it takes to locate a duck press will be worth it once you taste the succulent results.

Serve the pressed duck over a mixture of brown and wild rice, and broil the legs for a second course.

3 duck livers
¾ cup water
¾ cup red port
1 cup good-quality Cognac
5 mallards
Juice of ½ lemon
3 tablespoons butter
1 teaspoon arrowroot dissolved in
** 2 teaspoons water**

Preheat the oven to 425 degrees.

Cover the livers with the water and simmer gently until cooked, about 10 minutes. Reserve the cooking liquid, place the livers in a small bowl and mash with a fork. Stir in the port and Cognac.

Cut the legs off the ducks and set aside. Cook the ducks on a rack, breast side up, in the preheated oven, for 25 minutes. Carefully remove the breasts and cut them across the grain into ¼-inch-thick slices. Place in a chafing dish with the 3 tablespoons of butter to keep warm.

Crush the carcasses in the duck press to extract the juices. Pour the reserved cooking juices through the press to gather any leftover fragments.

Add the juices, the lemon juice and the liver mixture to the duck breasts in the chafing dish. Stir until it is thick and turns a deep brown color. This should take about 20 minutes. If the sauce does not thicken, stir in the arrowroot mixture. Season with salt and pepper.

Roast Mallard in a Clay Pot

Serves 2

This is one of the best methods I know for cooking duck. The clay pot releases steam which helps to tenderize the meat and at the same time keeps it juicy.

2 mallards
½ teaspoon salt
½ teaspoon thyme
1 medium-size onion, peeled and
  quartered
1 tangelo, peeled and cut in half
¼ cup vermouth
¼ cup orange juice
4 juniper berries, crushed
1 teaspoon arrowroot dissolved
  in 2 teaspoons water
2 teaspoons grated orange rind

Immerse a 2-quart clay pot in water for 15 minutes.

Wipe the ducks inside and out, with a damp paper towel. Rub the cavities with equal portions of salt and thyme. Stuff each bird with half the onion and half the tangelo.

Stir together the vermouth and orange juice. Place the mallards in the presoaked pot. Add the vermouth mixture and the crushed juniper berries.

Place the pot in a cold oven and bake at 475 degrees for 90 minutes. Remove the lid and place under the broiler for 15 minutes, to brown the skin. Transfer the ducks to a platter and keep warm.

Degrease the juices in the pot and pour them into a small saucepan. Add the arrowroot mixture and cook over moderate heat, stirring constantly, until the mixture thickens. Sprinkle the finished sauce with the grated orange rind and salt to taste. Pour the sauce into a warm gravy boat and serve on the side with the duck.

Roast Wild Goose

Serves 4-6

I used to roast a wild goose the same way I cooked a whole chicken until I heard about this unique cooking method. The bird is placed in a hot oven which is then turned off. The result is a perfectly cooked goose which is very moist—no small achievement for a bird that has very little, if any, fat in its flesh. If you have any goose left over, try making the Potted Game on page 65.

5- to 6-pound goose, ready
  for cooking
2 teaspoons whole thyme, crushed
1 teaspoon salt
Freshly ground pepper, to taste
3 tablespoons soft butter

Preheat the oven to 500 degrees.

Dry the bird, inside and out, with paper towels, then rub with the thyme, salt and pepper. Place the goose, breast side up, in a large roasting pan.

Rub the skin with butter and more freshly ground pepper, and place the bird in the preheated oven.

Turn the oven off and do not open the door for 1 hour. Remove the goose from the oven and carve immediately.

Roast Teal on a Crusty French Roll

Serves 2

There are three species of teal commonly found in North America: the green-winged teal, the blue-winged teal and the cinnamon teal. The green-winged teal is the smallest of all American ducks.

Teal are my favorite of all game birds. Their succulent dark meat has a very mild, delicate flavor and their crisp skin is equally toothsome. By serving teal on a French roll, every drop of the delicious juices is saved.

4 teal
1 lemon cut in half
2 tablespoons olive oil
4 sprigs fresh mint
2 lemons, quartered
4 French rolls, lightly toasted and split
4 tablespoons garlic butter

Preheat the oven to 475 degrees.

Rinse the teal with cold water and pat dry with paper towels. Rub them inside and out with half a lemon, then with the olive oil (choose one with as mild a taste as possible). Stuff each teal with a sprig of mint and 2 lemon quarters.

Roast the birds, uncovered, for 10 to 12 minutes, then slip them under the broiler for several minutes to crisp the skin. Butter the French rolls and place a cooked teal on each one.

Serve immediately.

Baked Goose with Ginger-Flavored Beans

This combination of goose baked with beans is a variation on a standard French cassoulet. Traditionally, a cassoulet is made with beans, goose, pork, mutton, duck and sometimes sausage. Cassoulet ingredients vary from region to region and continent to continent—I prefer to flavor mine with ginger, rather than the usual bouquet garni made of bay leaf, thyme and parsley.

1 pound Great Northern beans
3 cups chicken stock (see page 82)
2 cups water
1½ teaspoons salt
⅓ cup tomato paste
1 teaspoon dry mustard
1 teaspoon ground ginger
2 cloves garlic, crushed
½ teaspoon freshly ground pepper
1 yellow onion, sliced
3-pound wild goose, quartered
¼ pound salt pork, cubed
½ cup breadcrumbs
2 tablespoons melted butter

Soak the beans overnight in a large pot of water. Drain the beans and place in a heavy flameproof casserole with 2 cups of the chicken stock, 2 cups of water and 1 teaspoon salt. Cook the beans over moderately high heat until they are barely tender, about 1 hour. (You may need to add more water as they cook.)

Preheat the oven to 300 degrees.

Add the tomato paste, dry mustard, powdered ginger, garlic, salt and freshly ground pepper to the beans. Stir gently to distribute the spices evenly. Place the onion slices in an even layer over the beans. Put the goose pieces on top of the onions, flesh side up. Place salt pork on top and pour the remaining cup of chicken stock over the mixture. Cover with a tight-fitting lid and cook in the preheated oven for 3 hours.

Mix together the breadcrumbs and the melted butter. Spread the breadcrumbs evenly over the top of the goose and bake at 300 degrees uncovered, until the surface is well browned, about 10 minutes.

The goose is a most useful bird, according to one 15th-century Italian writer, who commended it "for its feathers, which may be plucked out twice a year; from these we make pillows so that the necks of spoiled persons may rest more softly. We eat the flesh both fresh and salted, and many dishes are prepared with the fat. Its liver is especially fine if first soaked in milk or wine sweetened with honey."

Sautéed Goose Strips with Parmesan

Serves 4

This recipe can be made with Parmesan cheese or Sbrinz (also known as Spalen), which is a hard cows' milk cheese imported from Switzerland. Sbrinz is slightly tangier and considerably less expensive than imported Parmesan.

½ cup freshly grated Parmesan or Sbrinz cheese
½ cup breadcrumbs
4 tablespoons butter
2 goose breasts cut into ¼-inch slices
2 eggs, lightly beaten
Salt and freshly ground pepper, to taste
3 tablespoons chopped parsley, for garnish

Mix together the cheese and the breadcrumbs. Dip the goose meat in the beaten egg and then in the cheese mixture.

Heat the butter in a heavy skillet and quickly sauté the strips in the hot butter, for 2 or 3 minutes per side. Transfer to a warm platter, season with salt and pepper, sprinkle with chopped parsley, and serve immediately.

Roast Brant with Brandy

Serves 2

A brant is a delicious bird that is larger than a duck but smaller than a goose. There are two species, the American brant and the black brant. Both species nest in the Arctic and migrate in the winter to coastal bay areas in the United States where they feast on eel grass. The American brant lives on the eastern side of the continent while the black brant prefers the west.

2½-pound brant, ready
    for cooking
½ teaspoon salt
½ teaspoon thyme
¼ teaspoon freshly ground pepper
1 cup sliced mushrooms
3 tablespoons soft butter
1½ cups cooked brown rice mixed
    with 1 cup cooked wild rice
½ cup beef stock (see page 82)
1 tablespoon brandy
2 tablespoons chopped fresh
    parsley

Preheat the oven to 450 degrees.

Dry the cavity and flesh of the bird thoroughly with paper towels. Combine the salt, thyme and pepper in the palm of your hand and rub the mixture thoroughly into both the flesh and the cavity.

Sauté the mushrooms in 1 tablespoon of butter for 5 minutes, or until they soften. Toss the mushrooms with the rice and stuff inside the bird.

Place the brant in a heavy ovenproof skillet just large enough to accommodate it snugly and bake, uncovered, in the preheated oven for 35 minutes, or until the juices of the breast run clear.

Transfer the bird to a warm platter. Discard any grease that may have accumulated in the bottom of the skillet. Add the beef stock and brandy to the skillet and bring the liquid to a boil, scraping up all the cooking particles in the bottom of the pan.

Cut the bird in half with poultry shears and place on individual warm plates. Pour the sauce over both portions, sprinkle with the chopped parsley and serve immediately.

Baked Woodcock with Lingonberry Stuffing

Serves 4

We do not have woodcock on the West Coast, so I have never cooked one. When I do, I plan to use this recipe, which was given me by John Poister, noted author of New York *magazine's "On the Town,"* The Pyromaniac's Cookbook *and* Meals for Males.

9 tablespoons butter
1 cup breadcrumbs
Salt
Freshly ground black pepper
Pinch of thyme or rosemary
⅔ cup lingonberries, drained
1 tablespoon heavy cream

Preheat the oven to 300 degrees.

Heat 2 tablespoons of the butter in a large skillet and brown the breadcrumbs. Transfer to a mixing bowl, season to taste with salt, ground pepper and a pinch of thyme or rosemary. Mix well. Add the drained lingonberries and the tablespoon of cream to help bind the mixture.

Spoon the stuffing into the cavities of the woodcock

6 woodcock, ready for the pot
¼ cup flour
1 onion, finely chopped
1 clove garlic, minced
2 cups beef or chicken stock
   (see page 82)
1 cup dry red wine
⅓ cup Cognac

and sew the openings closed with twine. Truss the birds so that the legs and wings are held close against the bodies. Heat 4 tablespoons of butter in the skillet you used to brown the breadcrumbs. Rub the birds with salt, pepper and flour and brown them in the skillet over high heat.

Place the chopped onion, minced garlic, beef stock and dry red wine in a roasting pan, arrange the woodcock in the pan and bake in the preheated oven until the birds are tender when the breasts are pierced with a fork, about 30 minutes. Baste the birds frequently with the pan juices. When the woodcock are cooked, remove the twine and place them on a heated platter. Keep hot.

Place the roasting pan on top of the stove and boil the juices to reduce slightly.

Blend 3 tablespoons of butter with 2 tablespoons of flour in a heavy-bottomed saucepan and cook over moderate heat until the flour is lightly browned. Remove the saucepan from the heat and cool slightly. Strain the juices from the roasting pan through a sieve and very gradually add to the roux in the saucepan, stirring constantly, until the sauce is thick, creamy and smooth.

Arrange the woodcock on a heated flameproof platter. Warm the Cognac in a small saucepan, ignite and pour the flames, very slowly, over the birds. Pour the hot sauce over the woodcock and serve immediately.

GAME CHARCUTERIE

Strictly speaking, a charcuterie is a shop that specializes in cooked meats. The term used to refer to shops that sold pork products only, but today it is used loosely to include sausages, pâtés, terrines and foie gras, to name but a few of the items now described as charcuterie.

An entire book could be written on charcuterie products made with game. I have included here one of my special favorites: goose liver pâté made with wild goose liver—it is sinfully delicious. If you don't like wild goose, give the bird away to someone who does, but be sure to keep the liver!

Game sausages have a wonderful flavor and are an excellent gift for non-hunters. Many hunters who take their game to a butcher shop for cutting and packaging also have cured sausages made from the scrap meats. If you would like to make your own sausages, have the butcher wrap the scrap meat in 2-pound packages and label them as sausage meat, freeze the packages along with the rest of your meat and you can make sausages, fresh or cured, whenever you are ready.

Homemade game sausages are surprisingly easy to make once you have the essential equipment and ingredients on hand. You will need a meat grinder, a stuffer spout, casings, binder, an assortment of spices and herbs, and a curing agent, for cured sausage. To grind the meat, you can use an electric mixer which has a meat grinder attachment, an electric meat grinder, a food processor, or a simple, old-fashioned meat grinder such as a Universal No. 333.

One of the questions people ask me most often is how sausage made with the food processor compares with sausage made with a meat grinder. The food processor is wonderful for making a small quantity of sausage. I often use it when I want to make fresh breakfast sausage on Sunday morning. However, it cannot give you the consistent texture that the blade on a meat grinder provides, and it doesn't effectively deal with tendons or tough membranes.

If you plan to make link sausages, you will need a stuffer spout to fit a meat grinder with a screw handle. They can be purchased at kitchenware shops.

There are many different types of casings available, but they usually fall into two general classifications: natural and synthetic. Natural casings, used for fresh sausages, are made from the intestines of cattle, sheep and hogs, and are edible. Synthetic casings, used for cured sausages, are made from cellulose and most of them must be removed before eating. For homemade sausages you will need hog casings for fresh sausages such as breakfast sausage and chorizo, and synthetic casing to make cured sausages, such as Cured Garlic Sausage (page 71). For breakfast sausages I buy a salt-packed hog casing that comes in 1-pound containers, each holding enough casings for about 25 pounds of sausage meat. Under refrigeration, they keep for 4 to 5 months. The diameter of the casing is about 32 to 35 millimeters, or about the width of a quarter. Commercial sausage-makers use lamb casing for breakfast sausage because it

is small and tender, but I have yet to find a noncommercial stuffer spout small enough to accommodate a lamb casing.

Synthetic casings are available in two sizes. You will need a 2-by-24-inch casing for a 3- to 4-pound sausage and a 2½-by-30-inch casing for a 5-pound sausage. Synthetic casings come in several different colors: tan, amber and white. The color you choose depends upon what color or "bloom" you want your finished product to have. Synthetic casing should be bought prestruck—already pierced with small holes which allow air to escape during the stuffing process. Both synthetic and natural casings can be purchased through butcher shops.

Binder is used primarily to hold the sausage together. It improves the texture and slicing qualities of sausage meat and helps to reduce shrinkage. I use Heller's Bull Meat binder, which comes in 5-pound sacks and looks like soy flour. It is actually composed of ground corn, ground wheat, ground rye, ground oats and a specially processed rice. I buy it at a butcher supply house and, while it is not a necessity in sausage-making, I like the results I get with it.

Spices for homemade sausages can be bought premixed in 1-pound bags (also to be found at a butcher supply house), or you can

mix them yourself. I like to experiment with both. Whichever you use, just be sure that the herbs are fresh. Once the meat and fat have been run through the meat grinder and the spices have been added, fry a small sample to test your seasoning before you stuff the meat into the casings.

The second question people most commonly ask is whether they have to use nitrates to make sausage. There is no need to use nitrates if you only make fresh sausages, those that are stuffed into hog casing and are either frozen immediately or refrigerated and eaten within 5 days. If you plan to make cured sausage, you do need to use nitrates to prevent the growth of *Clostridium botulinum,* the bacteria that cause botulism. The interior of uncured sausages provides the perfect airtight environment in which the bacteria can thrive.

The curing agents, sodium nitrate and potassium nitrite, commonly known as nitrates, serve two functions in curing sausages. They draw water out of the tissue cells, thus preserving the meat indefinitely, because bacterial microbes cannot grow without the presence of water. They also "fix" the red color of the meat. Sugar is often used in combination with curing agents, to soften the hardness of the salts and add flavor to the meat. Many grocery stores now carry Morton's Tender Quick. Complete Cure and Complete Sugar Cure, both made by Heller, are available through butcher supply houses.

Cured sausages can be made by curing the meat before it is stuffed into casings, or by curing stuffed sausages in the refrigerator.

One other thing you will need to make any kind of game sausage is pork and if you wish, pork fat. Because venison contains practically no fat, a high proportion must be added to the basic sausage mixture. Pork contains a good portion of fat and that is what the following recipes call for. For an even richer sausage, I like to use a ratio of one-third venison, one-third pork and one-third pork fat. If you want to use venison meat, try a ratio of 80 percent venison to 20 percent pork fat.

If you decide to add extra fat, the type of fat you use is important. *Never* use venison fat, which has a strong gamey flavor. I prefer to use pork fatback, which I order from my butcher, because it has a firm texture. Fatback is not always available, however, so I generally use whatever fresh pork fat is available.

One of the nicest aspects of sausage-making is its relative easiness. All the recipes for fresh sausages found here follow exactly the same procedure, the only differences being in the seasonings. Once you have made Venison Breakfast Sausage on page 66, you can make any of the other fresh sausages by following the same method.

To cook sausages, place them in a skillet with just enough water to barely cover them. Prick them with a fork to let the fat escape and cook over high heat for 5 minutes. Drain and discard the water and cook the sausages over moderate heat until they are well browned.

If you add up the expenses of the "big hunt"—gas, bullets, beer and food—and then figure the economical value of making your own sausage, you will almost break even by the time you are through.

Simple Duck Liver Pâté

Makes about 1½ cups

Duck liver tends to have a stronger flavor than goose liver. The cream cheese and brandy in this recipe mellow its taste perfectly. Serve this as an appetizer or hors d'oeuvre with buttered toast or an assortment of crackers.

4 duck livers or 3 goose livers or 3 duck livers and 1 goose liver
¾ cup chicken stock (see page 82) or 2 tablespoons butter
3 ounces cream cheese
2 hard-cooked eggs
1½ tablespoons brandy
½ teaspoon salt
¼ teaspoon white pepper
4 lettuce leaves

Simmer the livers in the chicken stock for about 5 minutes, or gently sauté them in butter. Reserve 1 egg for garnish, then puree the remaining ingredients together in a blender or food processor.

Turn the mixture into a bowl or a mold lined with cheesecloth and chill for 2 to 3 hours.

Chop the reserved egg and line a plate with lettuce leaves. When the pâté has cooled, place it on the lettuce and garnish with the chopped egg.

Serve with freshly made buttered toast, or crackers.

Potted Game

Makes about 3/4 cup

If you ever find yourself with bits and pieces of leftover cooked game, do not despair. Game mixed with butter and fresh herbs makes a delicious spread for crackers or thin slices of dark bread. Pheasant, duck, rabbit and venison all make excellent potted game.

½ cup cooked game meat, boned
4 tablespoons cold butter
1 teaspoon chopped fresh chives or scallion
Salt and pepper, to taste

Place all of the ingredients in the bowl of a food processor fitted with the steel chopping blade. Process until the mixture is homogeneous. Season with salt and pepper. Pack the mixture into a small crock and chill for several hours or overnight.

Serve at room temperature.

Venison Breakfast Sausage

Makes 6 pounds

For a memorable breakfast, serve these venison sausages with sourdough pancakes smothered with fresh blueberries and sour cream. Your guests will compliment you for years to come.

The instructions given here are the "master procedure," to be followed in making this and the following sausage recipes—and any variations on them that you invent.

10 pieces salt-packed hog's casing
2 pounds venison, cut into
  1-inch cubes
4 pounds pork butt or
  shoulder cut into 1-inch cubes
½ cup water
⅓ cup binder (optional) (see
  page 63)
2 tablespoons powdered sage
2 teaspoons nutmeg
1 teaspoon cayenne pepper
1½ tablespoons salt
2½ teaspoons pepper
½ cup water

Soak the casings in warm water for about 15 minutes to make them soft and pliable.

Grind together the venison and pork, using the coarse (3/16-inch) blade of a meat grinder; or chop for 12 seconds, using the steel blade of a food processor. Add the rest of the ingredients and mix until well blended. Place the mixture in the freezer to chill slightly while you fry a small patty to check the seasoning.

Remove the blade and plate from the meat grinder and attach the sausage stuffer spout. Gently run warm water through each casing to remove any remaining salt. Gently pull the casing onto the stuffer spout.

Run the sausage mixture through the meat grinder until it reaches the outside end of the stuffer spout. Tie a knot in the free end of the casing. (If you tie a knot in the casing *before* the meat is run through the grinder, air will be trapped in the casing, blowing it up like a balloon.)

Continue stuffing the mixture into the casing. Tie with string or twist the sausages at about 3-inch intervals. If you twist the sausages, alternate the direction of the twisting: that is, twist the first sausage 4 turns to the right and the second sausage 4 turns to the left, and so on. This will keep the links from coming undone.

To store the sausages, either freeze them immediately or keep refrigerated and use within 5 days.

American Chorizo

Makes 6 pounds

Chorizo is a type of spicy garlic sausage that originated in the Basque country of Spain. I call this recipe American Chorizo because I have substituted venison for a portion of the pork, which makes it less authentic, but equally delicious.

8-10 pieces salt-packed
   hog's casing
2 pounds venison, cut into
   1-inch cubes
4 pounds pork, cut into
   1-inch cubes
4 medium-size altadena chili
   peppers, seeded, or 2 4-ounce
   cans chopped jalapeño chili
   peppers, drained
⅓ cup binder (see page 63)
¼ cup wine vinegar
4 tablespoons chili powder
1 tablespoon oregano
8 cloves garlic
1½ tablespoons salt
2½ teaspoons black pepper
1 teaspoon ground cumin

Follow the directions for Venison Breakfast Sausage on page 66.

An oldtimer, quoted in the Oregon Journal *in 1927, recalls his past:*

"I always had pocket money, for I got 15 cents a pound for winter deer skins, and 25 cents for summer skins. When I was in my late teens and early twenties, William Toner, the express manager on the Albany & Yaquima train, paid me 5 cents a pound for deer meat. A good buck would bring me $5 to $6. He sold them to the hotels and markets in Portland. I used to kill 50 to 100 deer a year. Pretty soon they began enforcing the law on the open season, so we could only ship deer meat during the open season, but there was no limit to the number you could kill."

Fresh Italian Sausage

Makes 6 pounds

This sausage can be eaten on pizzas, or grilled and served with fresh pasta and a green salad. Its characteristic flavor comes from the anise-flavored fennel seed, which is a native European herb. The bright feathery green leaves of the fennel plant and its stalks are used in fish cookery, and the bulb is eaten as a vegetable.

8-10 pieces salt-packed hog's casing
2 pounds venison, cut into 1-inch cubes
4 pounds pork, cut into 1-inch cubes
⅓ cup binder (optional) (see page 63)
¼ cup water
1 onion
4 cloves garlic
2 tablespoons chili powder
1½ tablespoons salt
1 tablespoon fennel seeds
2½ teaspoons pepper
2 teaspoons paprika
1 teaspoon cayenne pepper

Follow the directions for Venison Breakfast Sausage on page 66.

German-Style Sausage (BRAUTZCHE)

Makes 6 pounds

Brautzche is a spicy German sausage that is reminiscent of the beer sausages often served in taverns. It is called beer sausage not because it is made with beer or cooked in beer, but because it is so spicy that it has to be accompanied by a tall glass of ice-cold beer.

8-10 pieces salt-packed
 hog's casing
2 pounds venison, cut into
 1-inch cubes
4 pounds pork cut into
 1-inch cubes
⅓ cup binder (optional)
 (see page 63)
1½ tablespoons salt
6 cloves garlic
4 teaspoons allspice
1 tablespoon black pepper
2 teaspoons paprika

Follow the directions for Venison Breakfast Sausage on page 66.

Pheasant Sausage

Makes 1 pound

This delicately flavored sausage should be sautéed slowly in butter over low heat. Stuff this sausage into casings or shape it into patties. It is also good served with Madeira Sauce (page 83).

1 piece salt-packed
 hog's casing
¼ cup breadcrumbs
2 egg whites
½ pound raw pheasant meat, cut
 into 1-inch cubes
½ pound pork butt or shoulder,
 cut into 1-inch cubes
2 tablespoons chives, minced
¼ cup chopped parsley
½ teaspoon ground nutmeg
¾ teaspoon salt
¼ teaspoon white pepper

Soak the hog's casing in warm water for 15 minutes.

Grind the breadcrumbs finely in a food processor fitted with the steel blade. Add the egg whites and process for 5 seconds. Add the remaining ingredients and process for 45 seconds to 1 minute, until the meat is ground finely.

Fry a small patty to check the seasoning.

Stuff into the hog's casing, as directed for Venison Breakfast Sausage (page 66).

"Red-Hot and Rollin' "

Makes 6 pounds

This recipe came into being on the afternoon of the 1978 National Basketball Association Western Conference Championship playoffs between the Portland Trail Blazers and the Seattle Supersonics. I think that the excitement of the event in our household particularly inspired its creation, for this is a spicy well-flavored sausage. (The Trail Blazers won and went on to win the World Championship!)

8-10 pieces salt-packed
   hog's casing
2 pounds venison, cut into
   1-inch cubes
4 pounds pork butt or shoulder,
   cut into 1-inch cubes
1½ cups water
3 tablespoons coriander
1½ tablespoons salt
1½ teaspoons mace
1¼ teaspoons cardamom
1 teaspoon cayenne pepper
¾ teaspoon ground cloves

Follow the directions for Venison Breakfast Sausage on page 66.

Cured Garlic Sausage

Makes 2 3½-pound sausages

This cured garlic sausage has plenty of flavor and a smooth texture, even though it does not contain fat.

4½ pounds venison, cut into 1-inch cubes
3 pounds pork butt, cut into 1-inch cubes
6 cloves garlic
2 cups water
4 tablespoons salt
2 tablespoons black pepper
1 tablespoon coriander
1 tablespoon curing agent (see page 64)
¾ tablespoon mace
2 cellulose casings, 2 by 24 inches (see page 63)

Grind together the meat and garlic cloves, using the coarse (3/16-inch) blade of a meat grinder; or chop for 12 seconds, using the steel blade of a food processor. Add the remaining ingredients, except the casings, and mix well by hand. Fry a small patty to check the seasoning.

Stuff the mixture into the casings, following the directions on page 66. Pack firmly to remove all air space. Tie the end of each casing with string and place the sausage in the refrigerator to cure overnight.

Smoke the sausage at 150 to 200 degrees over hickory chips for 4 hours, or until the sausage attains a pleasing color or "bloom." To finish it, boil the sausage until it reaches an internal temperature of 152 degrees Fahrenheit. To check the sausage's internal temperature, remove it from the water, untie one end and insert an instant-reading thermometer. It is essential for the sausage to reach this temperature to fix its color.

GAME PIES

"Sing a song of sixpence, a pocket full of rye; four-and-twenty blackbirds baked in a pie." This familiar old nursery rhyme serves to remind us that game pies are nothing new to the culinary world. They have been a staple of European cuisine for centuries.

When our forefathers settled "the New World," they brought with them, as a matter of course, their methods for making game pies. Once here, they often substituted local ingredients for the traditional ones, depending on what was readily available.

I like to serve game pies hot from the oven, accompanied by a large green salad and a hearty bottle of wine.

Baked Rabbit and Artichoke Pie   *Serves 4*

This dish is smooth, creamy and rich—those are the best adjectives to describe it. The slight tartness of the artichoke hearts provides a good contrast to the delicate and mild rabbit meat. I often bake this pie in a 2½-quart gratin dish, but a 9-inch deep-dish pie pan works just as well. If you wish to elaborate a little, decorate the top of the pie with pastry cut out in the shape of a rabbit, moistened with a little beaten egg so that it will adhere to the pastry top.

2 tablespoons butter
2 tablespoons flour
1½ cups milk
¼ cup dry vermouth
1½-pound rabbit, cut up
9-ounce package frozen artichoke
  hearts, thawed
1 cup freshly grated Parmesan
  cheese
1 teaspoon salt
½ teaspoon pepper
1 recipe Rich Butter Pastry (see
  following recipe)
2 tablespoons heavy cream

Preheat the oven to 400 degrees.

Melt the butter in a heavy skillet over moderate heat. Stir in the flour and cook for 2 to 3 minutes. Stir in the milk and vermouth and cook, stirring constantly with a wire whisk, until a smooth sauce has formed. Set aside to cool.

Place the rabbit pieces and the artichoke hearts in a gratin dish or pie plate just large enough for the meat to fit in snugly. Season with the salt and pepper. Cover with the cooled sauce and sprinkle with the Parmesan cheese.

Roll out the pastry just large enough to cover the pie dish and place it on top of the pie. Crimp the edges and cut a slit in the crust to allow the steam to escape. Brush generously with the cream.

Bake the pie in the preheated oven for 35 to 40 minutes, until the top is golden brown and the juices bubble.

Rich Butter Pastry

*Makes a single crust
for an 8- or 9-inch deep-dish pie*

This flaky pastry can be used for all of the game pie recipes included in this book. The egg yolk in the dough makes a firm, dense crust not easily penetrated by the cooking juices of the fillings.

1½ cups flour
Pinch of salt
4 tablespoons butter, cut into
  small pieces
4 tablespoons shortening
1 egg yolk
3-4 tablespoons ice water

Place the flour and salt in a deep bowl. Cut the butter into the flour until the mixture resembles coarse meal. Add the egg yolk and mix well. Sprinkle the water over the mixture, tossing it with a fork. Form the pastry into a ball, place it in a plastic bag in the refrigerator and chill for at least an hour.

To make the pastry in a food processor, place the flour, salt, butter and egg yolk in the bowl of the processor fitted with the steel chopping blade. Flick the pulse button on and off about 10 times, until the mixture resembles small peas. Turn the machine on, gradually add the ice water and process until the mixture begins to form a ball. Remove the dough from the container, form into a ball and chill.

Cook as directed.

NOTE: If the pastry starts to brown before the pie has finished cooking, cover it loosely with foil.

Pheasant and Cabbage Pie

This pie is good made with almost any kind of game bird, including fresh or smoked chukar, duck and goose.

The recipe calls for boned pheasant, but you can use whole pheasant if you choose to—just joint the bird and proceed as directed. It will be a little more difficult to eat, dodging the bones, but will taste just as delicious.

2 teaspoons butter
½ cup diced onion
2 strips meaty bacon, diced
8 ounces German sausage, cut into 1-inch pieces
4 cups chopped green cabbage
½ cup chicken stock (see page 82)
1 pound pheasant meat (meat from a 1½-pound pheasant), diced
Salt and pepper, to taste
1 recipe Rich Butter Pastry (page 73), chilled
2 tablespoons heavy cream

Preheat the oven to 400 degrees.

Heat the butter in a large skillet, add the onion and bacon, and cook over moderate heat until the onion is just tender, about 5 to 7 minutes. Discard all the fat.

Add the sausage, cabbage and chicken stock. Cover with a lid and cook gently for 8 to 10 minutes. Season the mixture with salt and pepper and let cool.

Add the pheasant pieces to the cooked mixture and place the filling in a 9-inch deep pie dish or 2½-quart gratin dish.

Roll out the pastry to cover the pie. Crimp the edges of the pie and cut two slits in the pastry to release the steam as it cooks. Brush generously with the cream.

Bake the pie in the preheated oven for 30 minutes, or until the crust is golden brown and the juices bubble.

Italian Game Pizza

Serves 4

This recipe puts to good use the last venison steak that is invariably left uncooked from the night before.

PASTRY:
1½ tablespoons dry yeast
   (1½ packages)
1 teaspoon honey
1 cup warm water (110 degrees
   Fahrenheit)
3 cups all-purpose flour
1 teaspoon salt

FILLING:
2 tablespoons olive oil
½ cup chopped onion
1 tablespoon butter
½ pound sliced mushrooms
½ pound uncooked venison round
   steak, ground
¼ teaspoon salt
1 teaspoon fennel seeds
1 cup tomato sauce
1 teaspoon Italian herb seasoning
2 cloves garlic, finely chopped
½ pound cheddar cheese, grated
½ pound mozzarella cheese,
   grated

Make the pastry dough by dissolving the yeast and honey in the warm water. Combine the flour and salt. Add the yeast mixture and stir the dough until it sticks together. Knead the dough until smooth. Cover and let rise in a warm place for 1 hour.

Preheat the oven to 400 degrees.

Heat the olive oil in a skillet. Add the chopped onions and cook over moderate heat for 5 to 8 minutes, or until they begin to brown. Transfer the onions to a plate, add the butter and mushrooms to the skillet and sauté for 5 minutes, or until they begin to turn golden brown.

Combine the ground venison, salt and fennel seeds in a bowl. Combine the tomato sauce, Italian seasoning and crushed garlic in another bowl.

When the dough has risen, punch it down and roll it out to fit a 13½-inch pizza pan. Brush the dough with the tomato sauce, sprinkle with the venison mixture and top with the cheeses.

Bake for 15 minutes, or until the cheeses bubble and turn golden brown.

Pheasant Turnovers

Makes 8 dozen

These delicately flavored sausage turnovers make an unusual and delicious appetizer. They can be made several weeks in advance and frozen until you need them. Freeze them individually on cookie sheets, then transfer to plastic bags for storing in the freezer. Bake the frozen turnovers on a cookie sheet in a 450-degree oven for 15 minutes, or until golden brown around the edges.

PASTRY:
8 tablespoons cold butter, cut into small pieces
3-ounce package cream cheese, cut into small cubes
1 cup flour

FILLING:
1 cup uncooked pheasant sausage (see page 69)

To make the pastry, place the butter, cream cheese and flour in a food processor fitted with the steel chopping blade. Process the ingredients only until the dough begins to form a ball.

Form the pastry into a ball, flatten slightly and place in a plastic bag. Chill in the freezer for 20 minutes, or in the refrigerator for 1 hour.

Preheat the oven to 450 degrees.

Roll the pastry out on a floured board to ¼ inch thickness and cut into circles with a 2½-inch cookie cutter.

Place a heaping ½ teaspoon of the sausage mixture in the middle of each circle. Fold the pastry over the sausage, creating a semicircle. Crimp the edges together with your fingers.

Place the turnovers on ungreased baking sheets, and bake in the preheated oven until slightly browned, about 10 minutes. I usually turn them over after 5 minutes to brown both sides.

SMOKED GAME

The art of smoking food is one of the oldest methods of preserving food in continuous use. No one is quite sure how this ancient practice began, but one interesting theory suggests that it was discovered in prehistoric times by a man who happened to find the remains of a large animal that had been caught in a large field or forest fire. He took what meat he could carry back to his cave and campground and shared it with the rest of the tribe. The meat tasted good this way, so he brought more of it back to camp. He noticed that the meat did not spoil as fresh game did, and soon he learned that when the leaves started to turn golden, it was time to smoke his game to store for the winter ahead.

Since prehistoric times we have refined our smoking techniques, but they still remain relatively simple: The food is first cured and then smoked. There are two curing methods, the simplest being a dry cure. This is just what

its name implies. The game is rubbed with salt and left to cure in a cool place for 6 to 8 hours. The salt draws the liquid out of the game and, because of its high concentration, discourages the growth of harmful bacteria. Sugar is often used in combination with the salt. It cuts the hardness of the salt by softening the tissues, and also enhances the flavor of the meat. After the allotted curing time, the food is rinsed in cold water and left to dry on a rack at room temperature; it is then smoked.

The other method of curing is called brining or pickling. The game is immersed in a concentrated salt or vinegar solution for an allotted time, and then removed, air-dried and smoked. This method has the advantage of being faster than the dry cure and the spices penetrate the food more readily.

Chemicals in the smoke itself coat the surface of the game and inhibit the growth of bacteria.

There are two methods of smoking, using either cold smoke or hot smoke. For cold smoking, the smokehouse temperature is kept low, usually below 120 degrees. The food absorbs the flavor of the smoke, but requires additional cooking. Hot smoke ranges from any temperature over 120 degrees up to 225 degrees. Called "smoke cooking," the hot smoke cooks as well as imparts flavor.

I use a small electric smoker called a Little Chief. It operates between 150 and 200 degrees. To determine the temperature of your smoker, check it with an oven thermometer. If it is electric, consult your operating instructions.

The best fuel for smoking comes from deciduous hardwood trees. Soft woods give off unpleasant-tasting resins. I prefer to use wood from fruit trees such as green apple or cherry, although many people prefer hickory. Try to use damp or green wood to avoid a direct flame on the meat. The wood can be in almost any form, chips and shavings being the most popular. They can be bought in bags at sporting goods stores.

To determine the length of time meat should be smoked, use a quick-reading thermometer. Venison and game birds should be cooked to an internal temperature of 170 degrees. After an initial smoking of three to four hours, wrap the meat in foil and cook it in a 325-degree oven until the meat reaches 170 degrees.

Successful smoking takes a little practice, and the first thing to remember is always to use good-quality pieces of game, never tough cuts. One good way to help develop your smoking technique is to keep a record of your accomplishments. The record should include the food smoked, its weight, the type of cure, length of cure, type of fuel and the length of time cooked.

Just as our hypothetical caveman grew accustomed to smoking his game in the autumn months, I also experience an irresistible desire to put my smoker to work when the leaves start to fall. The brisk autumn air would not be the same without the wonderful smell of slowly burning green apple chips and the satisfaction of knowing that I, too, am getting ready for the long winter months to come.

Jerky

The word "jerky" is derived from the Peruvian word charque, *referring to meat that has been cut into thin strips and left to dry in the sun. It is simple to make and provides a nutritious food to snack on. During the holidays I pack homemade venison jerky neatly into old-fashioned canning jars and tie them with a red ribbon to give as gifts to appreciative non-hunting friends. I prefer to smoke jerky. If you do not have a smoker, you can still make jerky by using liquid smoke and your oven.*

MARINADE:
½ cup soy sauce
¼ cup Worcestershire sauce
2 tablespoons liquid smoke
  (to use only if you don't have
  a smoker)
2 cloves garlic, finely chopped
1½ teaspoons pepper

3 pounds venison round steak or
  high-quality scrap meat cut
  across the grain into 1-by-5-
  inch strips

Mix together the soy sauce, Worcestershire sauce, liquid smoke, if you are using it, garlic and pepper. Pour the mixture over the meat, cover, and leave it to marinate for 1 to 3 hours at room temperature.

Drain the meat and arrange the pieces on a rack. Smoke the meat 8 to 10 hours at 150 to 200 degrees over hickory chips. If you do not have a smoker, put the meat in a 150-degree oven until it is quite dry, at least 8 hours. If you have a gas oven, the pilot light should dry the meat in 4 days. When done, the jerky should be brown, dry and hard.

Store the jerky in a covered jar or plastic bag. It will keep indefinitely in a cool place, and it freezes well.

Smoked Wild Goose

Because wild geese must fly for a living, they have very little fat. The texture and flavor of the bird is greatly enhanced, therefore, by marinating it in an oil-based marinade. Serve this delicacy as an appetizer with a mild white cheese and unsalted crackers.

3-pound wild goose, quartered
¼ cup safflower oil
¼ cup soy sauce
¼ cup brown sugar

Place the goose quarters in a shallow 9-by-13-inch dish.

Combine the oil, soy sauce and brown sugar and pour the mixture over the goose pieces. Rub it well into the meat with your hands and then marinate the bird, covered, for 4 to 6 hours.

Place the quarters on racks over the baking dish and let them drip dry, about 1½ hours. When dry, smoke them at 150 to 200 degrees, using either green apple chips or hickory chips, for 3 to 4 hours. Finish cooking the bird in a 325-degree oven until it reaches an internal temperature of 170 degrees (see page 78).

Smoked Pheasant

Serves 4-6 as an appetizer, 2-3 as a main course

Smoked pheasant makes an outstanding and impressive cold appetizer on its own. I also like to serve it hot as a main dish, like this, or with sauerkraut.

1¾-pound pheasant, skinned
   and split
2 tablespoons freshly cracked
   pepper
1 teaspoon salt
½ cup corn oil
Red Cabbage with Apples
   (see below)

Rub the flesh of the pheasant with the salt and pepper. Place the bird in a shallow bowl and pour the oil over it. Cover, and marinate for 4 to 8 hours or overnight in the refrigerator, turning every few hours.

Pat the bird dry with paper towels and smoke for 3 to 4 hours at 150 to 200 degrees, using green apple chips (see page 78). Finish cooking in a 325-degree oven until the bird reaches an internal temperature of 170 degrees.

RED CABBAGE WITH APPLES

1½ tablespoons safflower oil
1 onion, peeled and chopped
6 cups shredded red cabbage
2 Red Delicious apples, unpeeled,
   but cored and sliced
½ cup water
2 tablespoons vinegar
1 teaspoon salt

Heat the oil in a frying pan and cook the onion and cabbage over moderate heat until the onion is soft, about 10 minutes. Add the apples, water, vinegar and salt and cook an additional 20 minutes, or until the cabbage is just barely tender. Serve immediately with the smoked pheasant.

Chinese Smoked Wild Duck

Serves 6-8

Wild ducks smoked by this method turn a rich mahogany brown. Placed on crisp lettuce leaves and garnished with fresh orange slices, they make an exotic appetizer for an informal cocktail party. Let guests slice their own pieces, and serve a small bowl of tangy Chinese mustard on the side.

2 medium-size mallards,
   quartered
4 cloves garlic
4 scallions, chopped
⅓ cup honey
⅓ cup soy sauce
½ teaspoon dry mustard
Lettuce, for garnish
Orange slices, for garnish
Parsley, for garnish

Rub each duck with a clove of garlic.

Finely chop or crush the remaining garlic. Combine the garlic, scallions, honey, soy sauce and mustard in a small saucepan and heat gently. Place the ducks in a shallow dish and pour the sauce over them. Leave them at room temperature for at least half an hour.

Drain the ducks and smoke them with green apple chips at 150 to 200 degrees for 3 to 4 hours. Finish cooking in a 325-degree oven until the ducks reach an internal temperature of 170 degrees (see page 78).

STOCKS AND SAUCES

Not all game requires a sauce, but a few species, such as pheasant, benefit from being cooked or served with one. The essential ingredient in the creation of many superb sauces is a good stock, and, fortunately, stocks are not hard to make. The procedure is the same for making stock from either beef or chicken: The bones are simmered in water with herbs and vegetables.

It is not often practical to make a pot of stock for just one or two cups needed in a recipe, so I try to keep homemade stock on hand in the freezer. I generally keep chicken necks and backs left over from fryers in my freezer to use for stock. If I find I have run out, I have to rely on canned varieties, which vary in quality. When I use a canned one, I cook a few of the frozen chicken pieces in the stock for 10 or 15 minutes to give it flavor.

You will notice that I do not include recipes here for stocks made from game. I have made them from venison bones and wild duck and goose carcasses, but I find their flavors overpowering. If you wish to try one, substitute a few venison bones or a wild bird carcass for beef or chicken bones in the basic stock recipes that follow.

While a good stock is the basis for many an outstanding sauce, the classic sauces can be divided into two types: those made with flour or other thickeners and those that are emulsified. Flour-based sauces include both basic white sauce and basic brown sauce. They are made by stirring together melted butter and flour over heat to make a roux. A liquid is then added and the mixture is stirred until it thickens. You need to remember two things when making these basic sauces: Always use equal amounts of butter and flour for the roux, and two tablespoons of flour is plenty to thicken one cup of liquid. Flour-based sauces store well and can be made weeks ahead of time and kept frozen, or refrigerated for up to two weeks.

Emulsified sauces, which require more care in handling, are made by adding oil or butter to a mixture of egg yolks and an acid, such as vinegar or lemon juice. Mayonnaise and Hollandaise are probably the two most widely used emulsified sauces. Hot emulsified sauces, such as Hollandaise, should never be overheated, or they will curdle. They should be served immediately, or kept warm in a preheated thermos or double boiler. A food processor or blender is a real help when making emulsified sauces.

My favorite sauce for game is made by a very simple method called a reduction. Made in the roasting pan, the juices are degreased, then fortified with brandy and water, before being cooked over high heat to reduce the sauce by half. During cooking the bottom and sides of the pan are scraped clean of any crusty—and tasty—drippings. The reduced sauce is then poured over the game and sprinkled with fresh parsley, and the dish is served. A reduced sauce can be flavored with a few tablespoons of cream or butter, green peppercorns or capers. It is the easiest of all sauces to make.

Beef or Chicken Stock

Makes 1 quart

For a particularly rich beef stock, brown the bones under the broiler before boiling them.

**3 pounds beef shank bones,
    or 3 pounds chicken wings (cut
    into thirds), backs and necks
1 onion, peeled and sliced
1 carrot, unpeeled and quartered
1 stalk celery, quartered
½ teaspoon whole thyme, crushed
2 sprigs parsley, chopped
1 small bay leaf
Cold water to cover**

Place the ingredients in a large pot and bring to a boil. Simmer, uncovered, over low heat for 4 hours. During the first half hour, skim off any foam that appears on the surface.

Cool the stock, degrease and strain.

Hunter's Brown Sauce

Makes 1 cup

This rich brown sauce is a perfect accompaniment for the flavorful dark meat of large game animals. It complements any venison dish, particularly Big Game Hash (page 25), Venison Steak with Cracked Pepper (page 27) and Barbecued Backstrap (page 26), and is delicious served over accompanying noodles or rice. Cloak the venison with the sauce, or serve it in a gravy boat alongside.

2 tablespoons butter
2 tablespoons flour
¾ cup dry red wine
1 tablespoon dry sherry
¾ cup beef stock
4 tablespoons tomato paste
2 cloves garlic
½ teaspoon whole tarragon, crushed
Salt and pepper, to taste

Heat the butter in a saucepan. Stir in the flour and cook over moderate heat for 2 to 3 minutes, stirring constantly.

Add the red wine, sherry and beef stock and stir constantly with a wire whisk, until the mixture thickens. Stir in the tomato paste, garlic and tarragon, and season with salt and pepper to taste.

Madeira Sauce

Makes 3/4 cup

This reduced sauce is light and should be served with mild-tasting game such as pheasant or quail. Try it with Pheasant Baked in Phyllo Pastry (page 38), Pheasant Sausage (page 69), Broiled Squab (page 48) or Mustard Rabbit Baked in Rock Salt (page 33).

2 tablespoons butter
2 tablespoons chopped shallots or scallions
2 tablespoons chopped carrot
1½ cups plus 1 tablespoon Madeira
½ teaspoon thyme, crushed
1 teaspoon cornstarch
2 tablespoons heavy cream
Salt and pepper, to taste

Heat the butter in a saucepan. Add the shallots and carrots and cook gently for 5 minutes.

Add the 1½ cups of Madeira and the thyme and cook over high heat to reduce the mixture by half. Strain into another saucepan.

Mix the remaining tablespoon of the Madeira with the cornstarch and stir it into the sauce. Add the cream and season with salt and pepper.

Hollandaise Sauce

Makes 1 cup

Hollandaise is one of the classic French emulsified sauces that goes well with light meat game such as pheasant and partridge.

1½ teaspoons lemon juice
⅛ teaspoon salt
1 tablespoon hot water
2 egg yolks
Few grains cayenne pepper
8 tablespoons hot melted butter

Warm the container of a food processor or blender with warm water, then dry. Add the lemon juice, salt, water, eggs and pepper to the bowl and begin processing. After 30 seconds, slowly start adding the hot butter. Continue adding the butter gradually as the sauce thickens.

Serve immediately or keep warm in a double boiler or thermos.

Béarnaise Sauce

Makes 1 cup

Similar to Hollandaise in both method and basic composition. Béarnaise is flavored with tarragon and shallots and goes especially well with dark game meat. Try it with Venison Steak with Cracked Pepper (page 27) and Barbecued Backstrap (page 26).

3 tablespoons chopped shallots
   or scallions (white part only)
3 tablespoons red wine vinegar
½ teaspoon dried whole tarragon,
   crushed
⅛ teaspoon salt
1 tablespoon hot water
2 egg yolks
Few grains cayenne pepper
8 tablespoons butter, melted

Boil the shallots, vinegar and tarragon in a small pan until the liquid has reduced to 1 tablespoon. Strain and set aside.

Warm the container of a food processor or a blender with warm water, then dry. Add the shallot mixture, salt, water, eggs and pepper to the bowl and begin processing. After 30 seconds, slowly start adding the hot butter. Continue adding the butter gradually as the sauce thickens.

Serve immediately or keep warm in a double boiler or thermos.